Natural Terrariums

Complete Herp Care

Philip Purser

For my wife, Jennifer, whose faith has been "a light in dark places when all other lights go out," and for Professor Randy Hendricks, a friend and scholar who continues to inspire.
Thanks.

Natural Terrariums

Project Team
Editor: Thomas Mazorlig
Copy Editor: Stephanie Fornino
Cover Design: Mary Ann Kahn
Design: Mary Ann Kahn

T.F.H. Publications
President/CEO: Glen S. Axelrod
Executive Vice President: Mark E. Johnson
Publisher: Christopher T. Reggio
Production Manager: Kathy Bontz

T.F.H. Publications, Inc.
One TFH Plaza
Third and Union Avenues
Neptune City, NJ 07753

Printed and bound in China,
07 08 09 10 11   1 3 5 7 9 8 6 4 2

Library of Congress Cataloging-in-Publication Data
Natural terrariums : a complete guide to the design and maintenance of herp habitats / Philip Purser.
    p. cm.
Includes bibliographical references and index.
ISBN 978-0-7938-2891-3 (alk. paper)
1. Reptiles as pets 2. Amphibians as pets. 3. Terrariums. I. Title.
SF459.R4P87 2007
639.3'9—dc22
                    2007003981

The Leader In Responsible Animal Care For Over 50 Years!™
www.tfh.com

Table of Contents

What Is a Natural Terrarium?

If you've ever been to the zoo and seen a venomous bushmaster slithering slowly through the palm fronds and fallen leaves of its habitat, or if you've ever strolled through your local pet shop and stopped to peer into the steamy, tropical environment of a giant day gecko, then you've seen a naturalistic terrarium. If you are like me and you've been keeping herps (herps is a term for reptiles and amphibians collectively) or invertebrates (tarantulas, scorpions, centipedes, etc.) for a long time, then you've probably even constructed a naturalistic terrarium at one time or another. The good news is that virtually all species of reptiles or amphibians that are available for purchase can be housed in some type of

The even better news is that building a naturalistic terrarium may be a lot easier than you think. With just a little know-how, even a beginner can create a living, growing, and biologically accurate desert or forest environment. And if you're a little more experienced at herp keeping, you may wish to challenge yourself by constructing a fully functioning swamp biome, complete with decaying peat layer, flowing water, living water lilies, and a reproducing population of prey fishes for your mud turtle or tiger salamander larva to dine upon.

I view herp keeping as a science, an art, and a mission. As for the artistic side of the hobby, I feel that the species we keep and the manner in which we keep them are reflective of ourselves and our places in the world. Many hobbyists put forth great effort in their endeavors to make a terrarium all it can be—like a 10-gallon (38 l) tank becoming a tiny microcosm sitting right atop the coffee table. A beautiful terrarium that houses a healthy pet herp is an awesome accomplishment.

Finally, I am an ecologist on a mission. The preservation of the natural world is one of my top priorities in life, and I try to do all that I can to keep the world as green and alive as possible. I would like nothing more than to spread that love of and appreciation for nature with my readers.

But enough about me and my philosophies. If you've read this far, you're obviously interested in learning more about just what a naturalistic terrarium is and how to construct one. And if this is true, you've come to the right place, because I've written this book to start off as general as possible. It will teach you all about the different components of the naturalistic terrarium (the substrate, the water, the plants, the rocks, etc.); then it will bring all of this basic knowledge together into a guideline for building any style of naturalistic terrarium you can imagine. By starting off on the ground level and working upward, this book will give you a solid working knowledge of virtually every aspect of the living terrarium.

Naturalistic terrariums are a complex style of terrarium that supply their inhabitants with many or all of the natural components that they would normally encounter in the wild. For example, a corn snake will thrive in a glass-walled tank with paper towel or newspaper substrate and a black plastic hide box, but it will not behave as it would in nature, for rarely does a wild corn snake seek out a home of paper towels and plastic boxes. Corn snakes dwell naturally in forests and lowlands, living in tree hollows and shady, peaceful groves. By constructing a terrarium that supplies your corn snake with some or all of these components, you will be able to witness your pet living and behaving almost exactly as it would in nature: hiding beneath slabs of bark, stalking its prey through a cluster of ferns, or basking amid the tangles of a gnarled tree branch.

The same holds true for almost any species of reptile or amphibian you can think of. While it may be able to survive in a tank outfitted with only the basic necessities of life, it will not live and act as it would in nature—as it *naturally* would. Naturalistic terrariums serve not only to allow herpers to have an infinitely more interesting and spellbinding experience with our pets, but they also radically improve the standard of living for our pets.

There is a naturalistic terrarium to fit every hobbyist, every herp, and every budget. The key is finding the right combination to suit your needs. That's where this book comes in. In writing it, I'm trying to keep all hobbyists in mind. I don't want the novice hobbyist to be overwhelmed with too much advanced information and techniques, but at the same time, I don't want to bore my advanced readers by providing only the most basic facts and figures on the naturalistic terrarium. Instead, I intend this text to be a usable, fully functioning resource text. I hope it will answer the questions and fill in the gaps that so many hobbyists, at all points in the experience continuum, have struggled to overcome in their own naturalistic terrarium endeavors. And remember that the construction, maintenance, and keeping of a naturalistic terrarium is supposed to be fun! Hobbyists the world over wouldn't spend countless hours, dollars, and effort in building and maintaining these elaborate enclosures if they didn't derive a great degree of enjoyment from it.

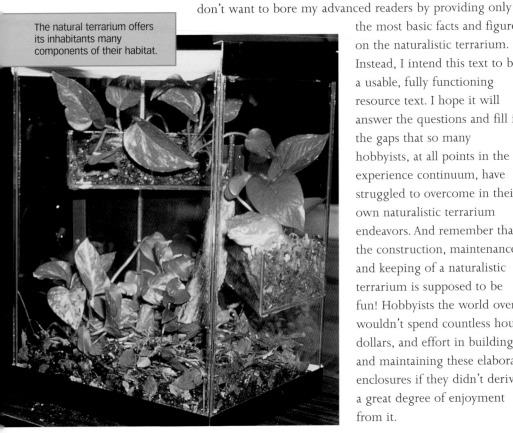

The natural terrarium offers its inhabitants many components of their habitat.

Chapter 1

The History of the Naturalistic Terrarium

L et's begin our understanding of the naturalistic terrarium through a definition of some terms. The word "terrarium," broken down into its Latin roots, is derived from "terra," meaning "earth," and the suffix "-rium," meaning "place" or "location." Thus, the terrarium is literally a "place of earth" or a "place of land." This definition is pretty simple to understand, because any terrarium meant to house an animal is, on some level, a contained portion of land or environment. But the modern definition of a terrarium isn't so closely aligned with the literal definition. When many hobbyists say "I keep my lizard in a terrarium," they may simply be saying that their lizard lives in a glass or acrylic tank outfitted with newsprint, paper towels, ground corncobs, coconut husks, etc. In fact, this is not a true terrarium so much as it is a low-maintenance habitat or Spartan enclosure. These sanitary habitats do function well as hospital tanks, quarantine tanks, and breeding tanks. However, when it comes to the long-term home in which your animal will live, I highly recommend using a true naturalistic terrarium.

The word "naturalistic" refers to nature: the plants, the rocks, the air, the sunlight, the water, and even the geological and biological processes that exist in nature. So a true "naturalistic terrarium," would, according to our definition of the phrase, be a contained "place of land" that incorporates many of the elements found in nature.

Terrarium or Vivarium?

Another term used in the herp and invertebrate hobbies is the word "vivarium," which refers to the complicated, fully living, ecologically balanced style of naturalistic terrarium. While this may sound pretty elementary, it is important to note that there is a slight difference between the naturalistic terrarium and the much more complex vivarium. A good way to think about it would be to say that all vivariums are complex naturalistic terrariums, but not all naturalistic terrariums are advanced enough to be considered vivariums. Hobbyists tend to use the term "vivarium" loosely, and it has become interchangeable with "natural terrarium."

Terrariums in the Past

Despite the recent surge in public interest in them, naturalistic terrariums aren't a new concept, not by about 2,500 years. As far back as 500 B.C., the ancient Greeks built contained, semi-indoor gardens for observation and for the practical purpose of growing various herbs year round. (These gardens were easily watered and irrigated during periods of drought that would kill field-planted herbs.) Similarly, the ancient Chinese perfected the practice of bonsai and of indoor water gardening purely for the aesthetic pleasure and spiritual enlightenment of the crafts.

Even in its earliest days, the terrarium was employed for both its commercial and artistic values. During these times, however, only the very wealthy could afford the lavish extravagance of an indoor ecoscape, because the working class commoner had neither the money nor the free time to dedicate to cultivating these self-contained gardens. It is believed that these systems contained only plant life.

Unfortunately, the naturalistic terrarium would not gain a foothold among the common populace until the middle of the nineteenth century. In 1827, Nathanial Ward, a British physician, was wandering the hills and scant forests just outside of London when he happened upon the chrysalis of a sphinx moth. Carefully plucking the cocoon from its branch, the doctor also scooped up a handful of earth and placed the earth, the branch, and the cocoon inside a covered jar, which he kept fairly moist. While he waited for the cocoon

Hobbyists often refer to natural terrariums as vivariums. Both terms are commonly used.

to hatch, Dr. Ward noticed that several small fern heads began growing out of the soil he had placed in the jar.

By the time the chrysalis hatched, the plants inside Dr. Ward's miniature conservatory had grown quite large and healthy. Marveling that the moth lived, despite the fact that the sealed jar allowed no oxygen to enter, Dr. Ward began to speculate that both animals and plants, if maintained in balance with one another, could exist in a closed ecosystem. As time passed and he dedicated more of his time and interest into growing plants in jars, the concept of the contained ecosystem began to evolve. After the 1842 publication of his book *On the Growth of Plants in Closely Glazed Cases*, word of Dr. Ward's invention, the Wardian case, quickly swept across all of England.

By 1852, the Wardian case, which was typically constructed out of an iron frame with glass walls and lid, was in use both by merchants and aristocrats alike. Tropical and exotic plants could now be imported from the world over without having to withstand the rigors of colder climates and salty breezes during a sea voyage back to England. The wealthy elite of Victorian England fueled this market for exotic plants and the continued production of Wardian cases. By the middle of the nineteenth century, almost every household among elite society owned at least a few Wardian cases, and as these cases became more and more a symbol of wealth and extravagance, the plants they contained became increasingly lavish. The cases themselves changed and developed into

Different Countries, Different Hobbies

While their popularity in America has spiked drastically in recent years, naturalistic terrariums have long been highly popular items throughout Europe and Asia. Hobbyists in these areas spend countless hours watering, fertilizing, lighting, trimming, and cultivating their vivariums. The act of tending to the vivarium is a very soothing, contemplative ritual that many hobbyists engage in to free their minds of worry or work-related stress. The end result is an at-peace hobbyist and a spellbinding vivarium. Most European and Asian hobbyists aren't shy about displaying their work, either. In many homes, the vivarium is the centerpiece, sometimes replacing the television as the object of the family's attention.

more elaborate structures based on the tastes and desires of their owners. Wardian cases, which were small and simple in their early days, were quickly evolving into more and more elaborate enclosures of greater sizes and different shapes. By 1873, the name "Wardian case" was replaced with the more appropriate term "terrarium."

It was not until near the end of the 1800s that people began heavily mixing both plants and animals within these enclosed biospheres. By the end of the century, European high society coined the phrase "vivarium," thereby encompassing all the "life" contained within the glass terrarium.

Modern Times

Sadly, the vivarium was pushed into the background of world culture during the dark days of the early twentieth century. World War I and economic depression meant that many people no longer had the time or money to spend on cultivating a vivarium. Not until the 1970s would these interesting curios come back into popular fashion. With the dawn of the modern conservation era came an unprecedented public awareness and concern for the environment and the natural world as a whole. Following closely on the heels of this development, both private collections and public displays of planted and inhabited vivariums once more came into fashion.

Zoos far and wide began replacing older cage styles with naturalistic, well-planted, and fully functioning terrariums of all sizes. Zoos that once housed miserable animals upgraded their facilities with lush tropical rainforests, vibrant flowering gardens, flowing waterfalls, and semi-complete ecosystems to accommodate nearly all the zoo's inhabitants. The 1980s saw the construction of tremendous vivariums, large enough to house giant pythons, bears, and even gorillas.

With the dawn of the 1990s, this trend in microcosmic environments surged forward. Public displays of increasingly elaborate naturalistic terrariums found their way into larger theme and amusement parks, shopping malls, and even local government buildings and business offices. As these public displays became more prevalent, the materials and knowledge necessary to construct vivariums became increasingly available, and the average hobbyist found it well within his grasp to construct and maintain a naturalistic terrarium within the home.

Today, the popularity of private vivariums and naturalistic terrariums is at an all-time high. Hobbyists all over the globe construct, maintain, and cultivate these tiny worlds within their own homes, and magazines and online sites post columns and feature articles dealing with some aspect of vivarium maintenance. And with such an influx of interest, the range and scope of these enclosed ecosystems have expanded accordingly, featuring room-sized terrariums with walk-in doors sporting adult Nile monitors; jungle enclosures filled with broad-leafed plants and crawling with poison dart frogs; flowing, filtered swamps under which lie submerged matamatas; arid, sun-baked sand dunes concealing Kenyan sand boas; and temperate forestscapes thorough which seemingly ageless eastern box turtles trundle.

Hobbyists far and wide create everything from desktop biodomes to room-sized mini-jungles. And the construction options are similarly diverse. Just a few clicks and a valid credit card are all that separate the average hobbyist from a custom-made naturalistic terrarium ordered via the Internet and shipped right to his door.

Originally, terrariums only contained plants, not animals. This continued to be the case until the late nineteenth century.

Chapter 2

Selecting
the Enclosure

The world of the natural terrarium is a spacious one indeed, and with so many choices and possibilities out there, it can be difficult to determine a game plan and settle upon a good starting point. The hobbyist has to ask himself so many questions before heading out in any one direction: What kind of herps do I want to keep? How large of a tank can my home or office hold? How much time and resources do I have to dedicate to my natural terrarium? Let's start at the beginning and progress until we've found all the answers and covered all the necessary bases.

Two Different Approaches

One of the best ways to start off your new natural terrarium is to first decide upon the species of herp you want to keep. Read all you can about the animal—learn about its origins, diet, and life habits before you begin building a home for it. Once you understand your animal's needs in captivity, you'll be ready to begin.

A second method of terrarium construction is to study a particular biome or region of the earth. This research can take you in very broad or very narrow directions. By "broad" I mean that the naturalistic terrarium might be described as a "swamp" or a "desert." These are general, catchall descriptions that encompass a wide range of features and naturalistic elements. For example, a generic swamp terrarium might incorporate 6 inches (15 cm) of filtered

Some hobbyist go to great lengths to accurately recreate their pets habitat, including using plants native to the area. An Amazon tree boa is pictured.

water on one end of the tank, a peat landmass on the other end, some floating plants, a half-submerged log, and an eastern tiger salamander inhabitant. In this basic setup, it really doesn't make a difference whether the tiger salamander and the water hyacinth are native to the same geographic areas or if the water column is alive with native fish species that the salamander might normally prey upon in the wild.

After a hobbyist gains some experience in dealing with the broad swamp habitat, he might want to help that habitat evolve into a more realistic slice of a specific ecosystem. For example, an Okefenokee Swamp habitat will contain components that are unique to the Okefenokee Swamp (an enormous swamp located in the southeastern corner of Georgia). These elements might include peat collected from the Okefenokee, acidic water of the same pH as that within the Okefenokee, a half-submerged length of a Virginia pine log, some water lilies, and several sundew and pitcher plants growing along the shoreline. An appropriate inhabitant for this style of vivarium might include a greater siren, a red-eared slider, a small mud turtle, a bullfrog, or a southern hognose snake. Such an area-specific natural terrarium often can take months or even years to fully assemble if you do not live near the area you wish to recreate and cannot readily (or legally) harvest your own materials. But once it's finished, looking into that microhabitat will be virtually identical to

Hot Herps

It seems that more and more hobbyists are keeping venomous reptiles of one species or another these days, so a word on these animals is in order. The cardinal rule of keeping venomous (or "hot") herps is security, security, security! While many commonly available venomous species fare well in non-naturalistic terrariums, most of these animals display considerably more natural behaviors (longer periods of basking, more movement, etc.) when housed in a living vivarium. But because these animals represent a potentially lethal event should one get loose or an unwitting child or friend open the terrarium lid, it is your responsibility to secure these animals to the utmost degree, both for the safety of the reptiles and the humans involved. Make sure that all lids fit very snugly into the framework of the terrarium; using a countersinking, locking lid is best. Also ensure that the screen is thick enough that your snake cannot burst through it; large pit vipers can be surprisingly strong.

At the time of this writing, I house a young southern copperhead, and perhaps I can give a good example of hot herp security by detailing my own situation. For starters, I have the copperhead's terrarium in my garage, away from the living quarters of my house, so that an escape will likely lead to the snake venturing back into its native north Georgia habitat and not into the floor of my bathroom. Secondly, I have the tank anchored to a shelf with bolts so that no one accidentally knocks it over and breaks it. Thirdly, the lid is made of a heavy-gauge wire base with a much finer wire atop it; this dual layering means that the snake can neither burst nor squeeze through the mesh. The lid itself countersinks into the frame and locks with a padlock, to which I have the only key hidden away. As a final measure of security, I have small yellow signs above the dead bolts on all the doors to my house reading: "Caution: Venomous Reptiles Present." This alerts any friends and family (or police or paramedics) of the potential danger within my home.

Bear in mind that lax security in venomous endeavors hurts everyone involved. Humans and other pets may be bitten and seriously injured, the venomous snake may be injured or killed, and other hobbyists may suffer if one keeper's accident causes local or state officials to pass new laws restricting the keeping of venomous reptiles. Remember, for the benefit of everyone: security, security, security!

peering into a small corner of
the real-life Okefenokee Swamp!

The Enclosure

The first step is to acquire or
build an enclosure, often an
aquarium or fish tank. The best
of these are manufactured to
serve as true aquariums; thus,
they are tightly sealed and hold
water perfectly.

Glass Aquariums

Although they are not the
only style on the market, I recommend aquariums that are

Glass aquariums are
popular choices for use
as natural terrariums.

constructed almost entirely out of glass (excluding the plastic trim
at the top and bottom), because glass tanks resist scratching, are easily cleaned, and allow
for maximum visibility of the naturalistic setup and all of its inhabitants. Most glass tanks
also can be fitted with a variety of lids, which will be important depending on which
habitat you construct. For example, screen lids are critical to arid terrariums, while partially
solid lids help to maintain high humidity in swamp and jungle environments. The only
major drawbacks to glass are its tremendous weight (all-glass tanks can be very heavy) and
the fragile nature of glass. If you plan to settle a large number of heavy stones in the bottom
of the tank, you run the risk of the base glass cracking or even shattering. Once broken,
glass cannot be repaired, and the terrarium must be broken down and re-established in a
new enclosure.

Acrylic Aquariums

The second major type of aquarium is acrylic. A sturdy, virtually unbreakable type of
plastic, acrylic will last forever, and a tank constructed of acrylic is much lighter in weight
than a glass tank of equal dimensions. Despite its durability, however, acrylic does have
several drawbacks that prevent it from being, in my opinion, an acceptable material for the
prolonged maintenance of the naturalistic terrarium. For starters, acrylic is easily scratched,
and should you house an animal with thick, heavy claws, it may scratch up the inner walls

of the tank through its regular movements. Similarly, if you establish a desert habitat inside an acrylic terrarium, you'll soon discover that the rocks and sand of the habitat can seriously mar the acrylic. Over time, these minute scratches can accumulate to the point that the acrylic takes on a frosted or sand-blasted appearance. This frosting will severely hinder the keeper's visibility looking into the terrarium, as well as the inhabitant's visibility looking out of the tank.

Another major drawback to acrylic is its porous nature. Unlike glass, acrylic has tiny pockets, nooks, and crannies in its surface, most of which can only be seen on the microscopic level. Unfortunately, the fact that they are so small is what makes these tiny nooks so troublesome. Algae are single-celled plant-like organisms. When they grow, their minuscule cells anchor themselves in any spot that will accommodate them, including the pores of an acrylic tank.

If you construct a swamp, jungle, or other damp habitat, as algae grow along the walls of the tank, tiny amounts will seep into the pores, where they will escape the hobbyist's brush when it comes time to scrub them away. Over time, these microbits of algae will fill virtually all the pores within the tank that are beneath the water line or the line to which algae grow. The acrylic will then, by virtue of its little green hitchhikers, take on a permanent jade to olive hue. This stained coloration is unattractive, and it severely limits the visibility of the terrarium and its inhabitants.

A final drawback to acrylic tanks is that their construction largely inhibits the use of multiple lids. Most acrylic tanks are designed solely for use with fish; thus, the lids are solid, allowing for minimal gas exchange

Many hobbyists recommend using front-opening, glass-doored acrylic enclosures for natural terrariums.

with the atmosphere. Because superior airflow is vital to the long-term success of most styles of naturalistic terrariums, a lid that inhibits this air circulation is a definite hindrance to the well-being and longevity of the vivarium. If opting for an acrylic tank, I strongly suggest that you purchase one of the varieties that is specifically manufactured for use with reptiles or amphibians, not the type made for fish.

Wooden Enclosures

One type of tank that you absolutely must avoid is the homemade wooden tank. While I had these when I was young, I cannot endorse their use under any circumstances as a naturalistic terrarium. Both glass and acrylic are perfectly inert materials. That is to say, they will never react to the materials that are put inside them. However, the organic walls of a wooden enclosure will react to whatever materials are placed inside it. Moist materials such as peat moss, most soils, pine straw, leaves, and mulch will hold some degree of moisture, which will rapidly permeate the wood of the terrarium. Once it is moist, the wood will begin to break down and decompose. This can lead to leaks, and eventually, the total collapse of the terrarium.

A final and very practical aspect of wood that makes it undesirable as a medium for constructing a naturalistic terrarium is its tendency to absorb odors. As your pet herp excretes, its wastes will emit various gases. Molecules from these gases will become trapped in the wooden walls of the terrarium. Even when all offending wastes have been removed from the enclosure, the molecules retained within the walls of the tank will still smell bad. As time passes and more and more molecules become trapped in the wood, the terrarium will give off a permanent funky odor, and no hobbyist wants to deal with that!

Size, Shape, and Style

Once you've settled on what type of tank you want, there is still the matter of what *style* of tank you want. The shape, size, and style of your chosen tank can make a big difference in the success you have with your chosen biome. For example, a 30- to 36-inch-tall (76- to 91-cm-tall) hexagonal glass tank would be an excellent choice for the hobbyist wishing to house a pair of rough green snakes in a deciduous forest biome. The height of the tank would allow the hobbyist to insert plenty of vertical branches, artificial or living plants, and vines. Because the rough green snake is a highly arboreal (tree-dwelling) species, it would be perfectly at home in such a tall, vertically oriented naturalistic terrarium. Arboreal geckos, tree pythons, and small iguanid lizards also might do well in such a vertical enclosure.

On the other hand, that same tall tank might be less suitable for the hobbyist owning a baby gopher snake. These snakes get large, and because they wander around in search of prey at night, they relish horizontal room in which to slither about. As a result, a longer, broader tank would be much preferred to a taller, thinner one in the case of the gopher snake. Large monitor lizards, turtles, small tortoises, and other heavy-bodied snakes may prefer longer, wider terrariums as well. So before purchasing your tank, you'll need to understand what types of herps that style of tank will best serve. Taller, thinner tanks are best for arboreal species, while longer, wider models are recommended for terrestrial or fossorial (burrowing) animals.

Another matter to consider is how the tank opens. Does it open at the top by way of a lid? Does it have sliding doors that allow for access from the front or ends of the tank? Either of these styles can be used to construct a naturalistic terrarium, but each has

Screened cages do not work for most types of natural terrariums, but they are useful if you intend to house chameleons or some other arboreal species.

its advantages and drawbacks. The open-top style is, in my opinion, best for very fleet-footed lizards and thin, small snakes. Lids constructed of plastic or metal with metallic or nylon mesh screening allow for excellent ventilation, and they help to keep small, ground-dwelling herps safely contained within the naturalistic terrarium. This style of opening is also best for natural terrariums that incorporate large amounts of water, as the sides and bottom of the jungle or swamp vivarium must be tightly sealed to prevent water leakage.

The sliding door style is an excellent choice for arboreal species such as geckos, as well as for very large animals such as monitor lizards and adult boas. This style of terrarium usually incorporates a system of sliding glass panels or doors that run in a track. Powerful species—those that could push a top-fitting lid off to escape—are much more securely contained within this tank style, because most sliding door tanks come equipped with some type of locking mechanism. Arboreal species, which naturally climb upward to seek freedom, often can find escape routes through insecurely fitted screen lids, yet they may never even look to the low sliding glass doors as a means of escape—the latter way out of the tank is simply not a

Provide Enough Space

The adult size and space requirements of your herp are major considerations when choosing a tank in which to establish your natural terrarium. If an animal is housed in a tank that is too small to suit its needs, then not only will your pet be horribly cramped, but the terrarium may also suffer under the weight of its oversized occupant. An adult savanna monitor, for example, can grow to lengths of 48 inches (1.2 m). A suitable terrarium, therefore, should be at least 72 inches (1.8 m) long and at least 60 inches (1.5 m) wide. This gives the monitor plenty of room to turn around and even walk some (although an animal of that size would definitely have to be taken out of its terrarium and exercised regularly). However, to house a savanna monitor in a naturalistic terrarium, you would need an enclosure at least double that size. To really create a semi-natural environment for your pets, you must provide as much space as possible. Clearly, it is easier to house smaller species in natural terrariums than large ones, but any herp can be housed in a natural terrarium, if you have the space and other resources.

natural route that arboreal species would take. I do not recommend that the sliding door style terrarium be used in the case of small, ground-going lizards or snakes, because the small gaps between the two sliding doors are often wide enough to allow small snakes, such as garter snakes and ribbon snakes, to slither out and escape into your home.

The sliding glass doors do not form a water-tight seal, even when closed, meaning that no form of water-intensive terrarium can be constructed if the water line rises above the bottom of the track in which the doors slide. Speaking of this track, it is also important to note that pea gravel, sand, and other granular substrates can easily build up in it over time and cause the sliding doors to malfunction or prevent the doors from sliding all the way closed. Many reptiles and amphibians have escaped from terrariums in which the doors did not slide all the way closed or seal tightly.

Herp-Specific Enclosures

In the past few years, a rise in the mass manufacture of specialized enclosures for the herp industry has occurred. A number of companies produce a few different types of enclosures.

Light, airy, "chameleon cages" may be constructed of nylon mesh woven about a large metal or plastic frame. Meant to provide the lizard with ample amounts of airflow, these

Given the space and resources, the only limit to the natural terrariums you can create is your imagination.

structures make very poor naturalistic terrariums for any species other than lightweight arboreal species that have claws that cannot penetrate the mesh. Good species for these enclosures include anoles, brown and plumed basilisks, and red-tailed green tree racers. Large or very heavy animals may tear the screen and escape, however. If you notice small tears or "picks" in the fabric of the cage, switch your animal over to another enclosure type. A few potted plants can be placed in the bottom of these enclosures, or live vines can be hung and grown within them. However, the overall effect does not satisfy the typical requirements for the natural terrarium.

The so-called "jungle terrarium" style of enclosure makes an excellent choice for the construction of a small naturalistic terrarium. Shaped like a glass cube, this style of cage has a solidly constructed lower half so that moist soil or water can be contained therein without leaking. The upper half of the tank is fronted with a pair of lockable hinged glass doors that open outward, allowing the hobbyist an excellent means of entry for cleaning, pruning, and maintaining the terrarium. And the top of the jungle terrarium is fitted with a locking screen lid to provide superior ventilation for the tank's inhabitants. Even though they are typically not very large when seen in retail stores (although larger models can be ordered from specialists), these tanks have a wonderful design that allows for the construction of a wide range of eco-scapes. These tanks hold water, so a swamp or a bog is suitable; they allow for excellent airflow, so a desert can be thrive in one; and their cube-like shape allows for a habitat that, to some extent, favors either height or width, so a tank of this type is equally suited to either arboreal herps or their ground-going kin.

Chapter 3

Substrates

As we've learned in previous chapters, there is virtually no end to the choices of materials that can be successfully employed in the naturalistic vivarium, and the hobbyist's choice of substrates is certainly no exception. Pet shops and online retailers sell a tremendous variety of substrates: ground corncobs, aspen chips, ground coconut husks, vermiculite, perlite, potting soil, pine bark chips, bark mulch, jungle mulch, and many others. The choices can be confusing; not all soils and substrates act the same, not all are chemically similar, and not all will work in just any old style of naturalistic terrarium.

You must choose a substrate that works well with both the plants and animals you intend to keep

Plant and Substrate Interactions

Before we discuss the various substrates and their qualities, the hobbyist must now face a big question: How will I plant my terrarium? If you will only be using a few live plants in your tank, you can probably bury the plant just to or just over the rim of its pot. This method of planting is very easily maintained. Simply water the plant by pouring water directly around its base. If the plant needs to be moved to another location or removed from the terrarium altogether, simply dig up the pot and replant it somewhere else. If this is the avenue you plan to take and no living plants will be grown directly in the substrate of the terrarium, your choice of substrates is not as critical. However, it's still very important to choose a substrate that will function within the terrarium biome you choose to construct and also meet the needs of the animal you will be housing within that terrarium.

If you belong to the other school of thought when it comes to the naturalistic terrarium, and you will be anchoring your plants, roots and all, directly into the substrate of your tank, you'll need to be very careful to select the substrate or substrate mixtures that will allow your plants to thrive and flourish. Choosing the wrong substrate at the beginning is a critical mistake that more than likely will result in the suffering or death of your plants. (There is a more complete discussion of plant species and their substrate requirements in later chapters.)

Types of Substrate

If your interest in captive life stretched no further than the flora of the terrarium, you wouldn't have to worry about anything more than how well your plants would thrive in your chosen soil mixture. But when you start adding the reptile and amphibian species into the equation, the chosen substrate type must satisfy the needs of both the plants *and* the animals you intend to house. If your chosen species of herp is a natural burrower, your substrate must be loose enough and light enough that your herp can burrow, for example.

Potting Soil

The first substrate that most beginning hobbyists reach for when constructing a naturalistic terrarium is potting soil. And while this almost instinctual move for the potting soil is understandable, it is also a mistake. Potting soils are formulated mixtures of organic and inorganic materials that are meant for use only in the plant pot. Potting soils retain moderate amounts of moisture, provided that they can drain exceptionally well, such as potted or hanging-basket style plants do. In the terrarium environment, potting soil allows water to pass through it to the lowest depths of the terrarium. This is good in that moisture doesn't stay high in the terrarium mix, but it is bad in that potting soil allows for minimal evaporation and wicking. (Wicking is a quality that allows that substrate to pull moisture from the depths of the tank up into the higher levels, where it can be absorbed by plants' roots, or even where it can evaporate back into the atmosphere.) Any excess moisture that is trapped at the bottom of a thick layer of potting soil will begin to fester, stink, and become an absolute haven for bacteria and fungi.

This inability to maintain a stable level of moisture leads to a secondary problem. As water leaks into the depths of the terrarium, any plants potted high in the potting soil substrate will soon begin to show signs of drought, such as yellowing leaves and drooping

Outside Soil—Just Say No

As tempting as it might be to harvest your own soil from just outside your home or garden, this is a critical mistake. Outdoor or "wild" soil may allow myriad plants and flowers to flourish outside, but it will behave very differently once you get it indoors. Inside the terrarium environment, outdoor soil tends to clump and harden, and it absorbs water very poorly. Any plants anchored in such soil will ultimately have their roots constricted and smothered within the compacting soil. Leave all outdoor soil in the great outdoors!

stems. So the hobbyist sees these warning signs and naturally adds more water to the tank. After a few days, the plants again appear thirsty, so the hobbyist again waters them—but all the while, the precious water is bleeding through the potting soil and collecting in a stagnant pool at the bottom of the terrarium. The end result of such a scenario is a sloppy, stinky mess of a tank in which virtually no plants will grow and in which no species of herps could ever live a happy, healthy life.

Potting soil often contains fungicides and fertilizers that make it unsuitable for use in a natural terrarium.

If this problem isn't enough to keep you away from the dreaded potting soil, I will warn you that many potting soils contain fertilizers, pesticides, fungicides, herbicides, or some other dangerous agricultural chemicals already in them. Designed to give gardeners and horticulturalists a helping hand when dealing with common greenhouse problems, these chemical agents can be harmful, if not fatal, to your pet herps. All species of amphibians, by virtue of their highly porous and semipermeable skin, may soak these chemicals directly into their bloodstream simply by sitting atop the tainted soil. Even the scaled and thicker-skinned reptiles are at risk, because many agricultural chemicals emit small amounts of noxious gases. As these vapors accumulate in the enclosed environment of the terrarium, they can cause serious respiratory damage to your pet, or they may accumulate in your pet's water dish and be ingested when it drinks. No matter how they enter the body, these agents may cause illness or death to your herp.

Despite all the potential problems it can cause in the naturalistic terrarium, potting soil is so commonly employed because it is readily available and very inexpensive when compared to more specialized forms of substrate. Don't let yourself be lured into this low price/convenience trap, though. Where is the value and convenience in saving a little money on a bag of potting soil but then losing a great deal more because you had to replace all the plants and tree frogs that lived in your jungle terrarium because of the tainted potting soil?

Peat Moss

Another substrate item that hobbyists frequently misapply is peat moss. Harvested from swamps, bogs, and decaying lowlands all over the world, peat moss is a highly acidic, organic form of soil that can be beneficial when used in moderation or when mixed lightly into another substrate. If used in excess, however, peat moss can lead to a host of problems.

For starters, peat moss retains amazing amounts of moisture. A handful of the stuff acts just like a sponge, so layering peat too deep in your tank can lead to a drainage problem. Plants rooted in perpetually damp peat moss may smother or rot if they are not accustomed to life under such conditions. Similarly, peat moss, especially when wet, can pack itself very, very tightly—so tightly, in fact, that pioneers, settlers, and Native American tribes that inhabited the Okefenokee Swamp in southern Georgia used to excavate huge blocks of peat from the swamp, let it dry out over the course of several weeks, then burn it for heat in the

Follow Your Nose

The substrate you use in your terrarium should become a living, thriving matrix of organic activity. As such, your substrate will have an odor to it but not one that is overly offensive. Active substrate will have a rich, earthy smell. When the odor of the terrarium changes radically, however, there is likely a serious problem with the health of your tank. Moldy, dank, musty, or excessively foul odors emanating from your tank are certain signs that the substrate is in need of help. Foul odors associated with feces or urine buildup can be remedied by spot-cleaning the substrate and removing the offending wastes. You can prevent these odors from forming by not housing too many animals for the size terrarium you have. Moldy or dank odors, however, may indicate that mold and fungi are running amok within the substrate. You can save slightly foul substrate by drying it out somewhat (by removing the lid and stirring the substrate every few hours) and adding living plants or a layer of decomposing leaves to the mix. If, however, the substrate is too sour, fetid, or overrun with mold, it poses a serious health threat to your herp. You must immediately remove it from the tank and replace it with a living, viable mixture.

Peat moss (shown here mixed with decayed wood) is a useful substrate when trying to create a swamp or bog terrarium.

winter. So dense were these blocks of peat that each one would burn in a fireplace almost like a solid piece of wood. Few plants that do not naturally thrive in such an environment could force their roots through such dense, inhospitable substrate.

Owing to its highly acidic chemical makeup, peat moss also has a bad habit of killing virtually all microscopic organisms that you'll need to cultivate in your substrate: bacteria to help break down old biomass, fungi to help your plants' roots absorb water and nutrients, and other such beneficial organisms. Peat is simply too dense and too acidic to allow these organisms to thrive in the home terrarium. Because the naturally beneficial organisms cannot get a solid foothold in the peat moss, biological activity within the peat moss substrate will continually be at a minimum.

Over time, small amounts of urine, feces, and other biological wastes will build up in the substrate. Without the bacteria and fungi to help break these wastes down into an inert form that can be absorbed by the plants, the soil can eventually become saturated with these wastes, rendering it and all the moisture within the tank highly toxic. These organic toxins present a threat to all amphibian life, because they will simply soak into the animal's skin and cause internal toxicity, which can kill an amphibian in a matter of days or even hours. Most reptiles will be somewhat more resistant to this form of toxicity; their first symptoms usually manifest as sores, lesions, and pustules along those parts of the body that are in constant contact with the tainted substrate.

Do your homework, however, before rooting some expensive tropical plants in peat, because the acidic pH is more than many species can tolerate.

Sphagnum Moss

When you need a light, airy material that can be used in virtually any style of nonarid naturalistic terrarium, the best material to reach for is sphagnum moss. Sphagnum moss is very similar to peat moss, and some forms of peat moss actually derive from decomposing sphagnum. When it is fresh and young, however, sphagnum moss isn't nearly as acidic in pH as is older, more thoroughly decayed peat moss. Sphagnum is a very lightweight, coarse material that allows for plenty of air circulation and almost perfect water drainage—the fronds of the sphagnum retain water, while the gaps and nooks between the gnarled fronds allow excess water to drain away. Orchids and bromeliads do especially well when anchored in sphagnum moss, as do a wide variety of other jungle and forest plants. By simply misting the sphagnum around the roots of the plant every other day, you can supply plenty of water to those plants that need a little more moisture than the rest of the terrarium. So if I use sphagnum moss around the root system of a moisture-loving plant, I can maintain that plant and meet its moisture needs in a terrarium that is largely dedicated to plant species that do not need as much moisture. For this reason, sphagnum is commonly used in small amounts around only those plant species that need it, rather than being used throughout the entire tank. Think of sphagnum moss as a garnish atop the substrate of your terrarium; it works best when it is used locally and in small amounts.

The only drawbacks to sphagnum are its exorbitant price and its relative rarity in the open market. Sphagnum is typically harvested from the wild in a unsustainable manner, so

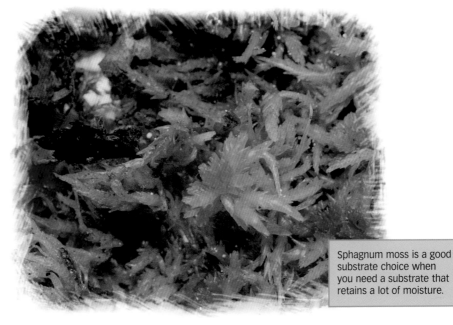

Sphagnum moss is a good substrate choice when you need a substrate that retains a lot of moisture.

the world's reserves of sphagnum are being harvested at a rate faster than they can be replenished. Because of this, some "imposter" mosses are often packaged and sold as sphagnum. Most of these imposters are some variety of sheet moss, which works well with some plant species, but which can be toxic to many carnivorous plant species of the genus *Sarracenia*. When purchasing sphagnum, make sure that you're getting the real thing and not one of the myriad imposter mosses.

Vermiculite

Valued for its extremely light weight, airiness, and ability to retain just the right amount of water, vermiculite is very popular among horticulturalists and professional reptile breeders. Vermiculite is perhaps the best medium for hatching reptile eggs. In the naturalistic vivarium, however, vermiculite retains too much water and may smother plant roots. It also has one of the shortest "shelf lives" of all terrarium substrates, breaking down very rapidly into a thick, almost clay-like substance in which virtually no plants will grow. Very old vermiculite that has compacted for a long time may form a solid brick when removed from a terrarium. Tiny amounts of vermiculite can, however, be beneficial. As it breaks down, it releases trace amounts of magnesium and potassium, both of which are essential to superior plant growth, into the substrate. Mixing a small amount of vermiculite into another substrate can be a good way to supply your plants with these valuable trace elements.

Perlite

Another substrate that is off-limits when it comes to terrarium use is perlite. Perlite is another light, airy material that horticulturists use, but it is much akin to charcoal in that it serves absolutely no viable function within the naturalistic terrarium. It merely takes up the precious space that could be filled with a much more helpful substrate material. Due to its bright white coloration, perlite is an extremely unnatural-looking material that really stands out in the home terrarium. Don't use it.

Many types of amphibians thrive on a sphagnum moss substrate. This male mantella is guarding eggs laid in sphagnum.

Drainage Rocks

Although not critical in all environment types (a swamp, for example), drainage, or the ability of water to drain down from the upper substrate layers into a deeper reservoir inside the terrarium, can be highly beneficial in forest, jungle, and even desert terrarium habitats. Establish a draining system by placing a layer of rocks in the bottom of your terrarium roughly one-third as deep as the substrate itself. For example, if you have a 4-inch (10-cm) layer of viable substrate in which your plants will grow, a 1-inch (2.5 cm) drainage layer of rocks should suffice. Drainage is important because plants need water in the soil, but most cannot tolerate standing water surrounding their roots. Therefore, a layer of rock that elevates your substrate and allows excess water to drain away from the roots will allow for the proliferation of plants within your terrarium through the elimination of standing water. The best rocks to employ when constructing your drainage layer are lava rocks, because these porous hunks of rock are inert and are very slow to decompose.

Pumice

If perlite had an evil twin brother, it would be pumice. Pumice is a stony material that is widely used in potting arenas for increasing drainage and aeration in otherwise dense potting mixes. In the home terrarium, pumice's highly porous nature makes each grain a haven for bacterial colonization; urine and fecal matter may collect within the micropores in each grain of pumice, thereby harboring odor and harmful bacteria. To make matters worse, pumice is visually very similar to a wide variety of calcium-based stones, which many lizard and crocodilian species frequently ingest as sources of calcium and other minerals. While a true calcium-based stone will break down inside the reptile's gut, a chunk of pumice will not. Pumice will impact inside the gut, and if not taken to a veterinarian for emergency surgery to remove the blockage, the lizard or crocodilian will suffer a long, slow, and painful death. Never use pumice in the naturalistic terrarium.

Wood Shavings

Nearly every pet store stocks some variety of wood chips or shredded bark. While the right type of wood chips or bark used in the proper manner can have its usefulness in the naturalistic terrarium, some wood chips and barks should never be used under any circumstances.

Various wood mulches and bark mixes are mostly useful as components of a substrate, rather than as the whole substrate. Shown are hardwood mulch (top) and cypress mulch (bottom).

The first chip (this refers to any form of shredded wood—chip, flake, nugget, strip, etc.) to avoid is the bright red, intense-smelling cedar chip. Used primarily by mouse, hamster, and other small animal keepers, this powerfully aromatic substrate is excellent at masking any offensive odors emanating from the mammal's enclosure, thus minimizing cage cleaning on the part of the keeper. The source of this chip's powerful odor comes from resins within the wood. When incorporated into the naturalistic terrarium, these chips emit their resins into and pollute the substrate mix. The resins will not only function to kill the beneficial bacteria and fungi that your plants naturally need to flourish, but they also may soak into the skin of any amphibians that may be living in the terrarium, leading to intense discomfort or even death. Reptile pets are also at risk, because these pungent oils can cause irreversible olfactory and respiratory damage over time. Herps housed amid aromatic cedar or pine chips also tend to be highly stressed, refusing food, drinking very little, and perpetually trying to escape their inhospitable enclosure.

A whole host of barks makes excellent additions to the naturalistic terrarium. Orchid bark (named for its use in potting orchids—it is not the actual bark of orchids) comprises variably sized chunks of the bark stripped from various fir trees. A by-product of the lumber industry, this bark does not contain the harmful resins and oils associated with the inner wood of evergreen trees, even though it may have been stripped from them. Avoid redwood, pine, and eucalyptus bark, however, because they do contain heavy amounts of resins and oils. Harmless orchid bark is very slow to decompose; thus, it may be added into a vivarium substrate mix to add airiness and water drainage to benefit orchids, bromeliads, and other tropical plants in the jungle biome terrarium. If layered atop a denser substrate mix, orchid bark does an excellent job of helping the substrate retain moisture, much like surface leaf litter does on a wild forest floor. This is especially beneficial when growing mosses and ferns in a terrarium that requires a stable level of humidity.

Coir or Coconut Husk

"Coir" is the horticulture industry's name for finely ground coconut husks and shredded coconut fibers, and it is one of the best natural products to use in the home terrarium. Very coarse by nature, these husks are ground into a light, airy substance that is commonly sold in bricks or in blocks from local pet shops. Simply place this block in a bucket of warm water overnight to expand the coir to full size. Use a very large bucket, because even a small block of coir expands into a huge amount of product when it gets moist. Not only does coir do a great job of adding airiness to a mixture, but it also helps to hold vital moisture and allows for the uninhibited growth and action of beneficial bacteria and fungi within and around the root systems of your plants. In addition, coir is a bonding agent that helps to

How Do You Wash Dirt?

Many hobbyists may, for one reason or another, wish to wash the substrate before putting it in their terrarium. Sometimes too much liquid fertilizer has been added, or too much dust exists that needs to be quelled. Either way, the notion of washing substrate can be a daunting task. How do you wash soil without washing it away?

Here's the method that has worked for me for years. Begin by placing the material to be washed in a large, clean bucket. Fill the bucket with water and let the material soak thoroughly. If the substrate is merely dusty, allow the dusty bits, which will usually form a fine film on the surface of the water, to drain off by tipping the bucket slightly, thereby leaving the desirable material in the bottom. Once thoroughly rinsed, the substrate may then be poured into the center of a large, open towel or sheet. Fold the towel by twisting the ends, and keep twisting and squeezing the wrapped substrate. As you twist, you'll wring out more and more water. Continue until no more water drips from the towel. When you unfold the towel, you'll find that you have a nice supply of rinsed, dust-free substrate, virtually none of which washed away.

make a homogenous mixture of your substrate. This quality enhances plant growth and adds ecological viability to your terrarium.

One of coir's only drawbacks is that, depending on how and from where it was harvested, it can be high in sodium. Because coconut trees are native to the salty sea coasts of the tropics, a large portion of these sea salts remains in the coir after it is processed and shipped to your local pet shop. Excess sodium isn't good for plant growth, and it is a serious inhibitor of beneficial bacterial and fungal growth. The good news is that once you rehydrate and expand your block of coir, it can be washed (with the aid of a very fine-mesh seine) repeatedly and rinsed of any excess sodium before being added to the home terrarium.

Coconut husks also enter the substrate equation in another form: the coconut cube. Geometrically cut from coconut husks, these tough, long-lasting cubes grant more and better drainage and aeration to a substrate mix than any other suitable substrate item. They are a great addition to the substrate of the jungle terrarium, because they will help to make an almost perfect habitat for orchids and bromeliads. In naturalistic terrariums that house invertebrate pets (like tarantulas, scorpions, and centipedes), coconut cubes are an excellent surface cover choice. This is because burrowing species can easily move and manipulate them, and the cubes allow virtually all water to drain away from the surface while still holding just enough moisture to maintain a high relative humidity, which is critical to the success of many tropical invertebrates. Coconut cubes, like coir, should be rinsed and dried at least twice before placing them into the naturalistic terrarium's substrate.

Leaf litter is useful as a component of a substrate or as ground cover laid over the substrate.

Ground Palm

Another fine substrate addition that hails from the tropics is ground palm. Made from the ground bark and leaves of palm trees, this light, dusty substrate is valuable if mixed with a denser substrate, because it will add aeration to the mix if used in a moist or humid terrarium. Palm is also highly prized for its ability to cultivate colonies of bacteria and fungi, which aids the growth of your plants and the natural breakdown of wastes. If used in arid environments, ground palm helps to make the substrate lighter in weight and density, thereby making it more accommodating to burrowing species. Like coconut by-products, ground palm is very tough and slow to decompose. Some of the only drawbacks to ground palm is its relative scarcity and higher price tag than many other forms of substrate.

Leaf Litter

Perhaps the best all-around substrate for use in jungle, forest, or woodland terrariums is the decomposing leaf. Dead leaf litter found around the base of shrubs and trees can be one of the best, most ecologically beneficial materials you could ever add to the substrate of the naturalistic terrarium. Leaves naturally stack up on the forest floor, and they decompose at various rates depending on how deep within the layers they are situated. Leaves at the top of the stack are largely dry and are slow to decompose. Top-level leaves function primarily to shield the lower leaves from direct sunlight (which is lethal to many types of bacteria and fungi), and they help the deeper layers retain high levels of moisture. Leaves deeper down in the compost heap are darker, wetter, and in a more advanced state of decay. The leaves on the very bottom have broken down almost completely into rich, dark soil. Every autumn, when the trees shed their foliage, a new layer of leaves covers the surface and the composting cycle begins anew.

This cycle of composting leaves is a natural process that is vital to the forest ecosystem. Within the deeper layers of leaves live vast colonies of beneficial bacteria, fungi, and other organisms known as detritivores. Detritivores (the name literally means "waste eaters") are responsible for turning the chemical compounds trapped in dead items back into usable substances that can once again be absorbed by plants. If there were no detritivores, nothing would ever rot and all the nutrients on earth would be locked up in dead plants and animals. And that sterile, lifeless environment is exactly what the naturalistic terrarium is working against. By adding a liberal helping of composting leaves to your terrarium's substrate, you can seed the vivarium with the good bacteria and detritivores that are necessary to establish and perpetuate a viable, living ecosystem within your terrarium.

To Leaf, or Not to Leaf?

Not all types of composting leaf make wise additions to the substrate level. Some species are tough, long lasting, and add a definite degree of biological activity to your substrate. Good choices are hickory, oak, elm, birch, cherry, poplar, cottonwood, willow, holly, ash, crabapple, pear, and the small leaves dropped by boxwoods and privet bushes. Take care when using holly leaves, because some cultivars have prickly leaves that might be an irritant to heavy-bodied, terrestrial species or soft-fleshed amphibians. As they decompose, however, these leaves can quickly lose their bite. Of course, there are other leaves that should not be incorporated into the home terrarium. These varieties typically break down very quickly, or they may exude noxious chemicals that can damage or inhibit the biological activity of beneficial bacteria and fungi within the substrate. Leaves to avoid include sweet gum, sage, mesquite, tulip tree, maple, magnolia, eucalyptus, oleander, bottlebrush, and most nut-bearing trees. Avoid all evergreen and fir tree needles, unless you're establishing a terrarium that specifically needs them.

Aside from harvesting your own leaves from the wild (when harvesting, collect only the rotting leaf matter and not the true soil beneath it), you also may obtain composting leaves from hardware stores and horticultural nurseries. It is important to know exactly what you are getting when purchasing or collecting leaves, because various leaves and leaf species will react very differently within the home terrarium. If you are uncertain about a particular leaf compost or leaf mixture, ask the shop's horticulturalist or resident expert. Tell him your plans with the terrarium, and chances are he will be able to steer you in the right direction.

Sand and Gravel

A final type of substrate that deserves mentioning is sand and gravel. Although they will be discussed further in the next chapter, sands and gravels can be very useful in both desert and swamp environments. When used in a desert environment, sand will obviously be the main component of the substrate, although not all sands are created equal. Silica-based sands (such as the type sold for yard projects and for use in children's sandboxes) are very loose, sharp-grained sands. Aside from the construction of the sand dune or Sahara-style desert terrarium, these sands are basically worthless. Limestone sands—pale, chalky sands—and calcium-based sands are not viable options in the average living vivarium, because their alkaline pH will not accommodate most plant life. (However, if you are in search of sand that will radically raise the pH of the soil, one of these might be useful to you.) Instead, find sands that are mined from harder, natural stones, such as granite sands, sandstone sands, or even volcanic sands. These items will cost a little more money and typically are sold only by vivarium dealers, rock yards, and specialized landscape companies, but the added expense and effort are worth it.

Shopping for Substrate

While each of these individual components described in this chapter has its pros and cons in the home terrarium, few are sold specifically for terrarium use. The hobbyist often has to search from one nursery or plant farm to the next to find all the components he needs to construct a naturalistic terrarium. If you have the time and money, I highly recommend putting forth the extra effort in rounding up all the best terrarium supplies. If you are the one-stop kind of shopper, however, who likes to get all you need in one bag, you're going to have your work cut out for you. While there is seemingly no end to the variety and diversity of prepackaged substrates on the market today, I've yet to find a single bag that can do it all. Don't get me wrong—some of these bagged mixes are better than others, and some are downright excellent (remember to read the "ingredients" of each mix before purchasing!)—but not a single one of them is the perfect, stand-alone substrate. Simply stated, you must have a mixture of several different substrates to successfully establish a naturalistic terrarium in which live plants and beneficial microorganisms will thrive. Exactly which materials you use and how you set them up will be determined by what style of naturalistic terrarium you choose to establish. We will discuss which substrates are appropriate for different types of terrariums in the sections on those terrariums.

There are many types of sand to choose from, so carefully select one that will fit the needs of your terrarium and its inhabitants.

Rocks and Stones

B ecause they are a part of every environment
on earth, rocks and stones play a critical
role in both the chemistry of a particular
area and in helping to maintain the surface
and stability of that ecosystem against the
driving forces of water and wind.

Rocks are a natural feature of many herp habitats, and herps use them for shelters, basking sites, and lookout stations. A desert horned lizard is shown here.

The closer you follow nature's rules, the more you increase your chances of success in your own mini-ecosystems. This is why you will probably need to add some variety of rock or stone to your vivarium habitat. Forests habitats may have boulders or granite outcroppings jutting from the soil, which serve as dens and hideaways for temperate snake species. Deserts are liberally strewn with boulders of various sizes, atop which bask the sun-worshipping lizards and snakes native to that arid environment. Bogs and swamps have, at their base, layers of sand and crushed stone that act as a buffering agent to help to prevent flooding and maintain pH in that biome. So with a few exceptions, a simulated biome that is constructed without rocks or stones isn't a very accurate simulation of that environment.

The benefits of rocks and stones go far beyond their applicability to various environments, however. They are integral components in the lives many reptiles and amphibians. Herps climb atop stones to bask and soak up residual heat; they shelter under stones to escape predators or the scorching rays of the midday sun; they hunt amidst stones; and most snakes will scrape against the rough edge of a large rock to shed their skin. Similarly, many species of tree frogs gather on streamside stones to call and chorus at night, and aquatic salamanders and newts must take refuge under the flat stones of creek beds and river shallows to escape predators and hunt prey.

Last but not least, rocks and stones can add great aesthetic value to the overall appearance of your naturalistic terrarium. A large, flat piece of slate can make an attractive basking stone atop which your California kingsnake could soak up some heat, just as a scattering of rounded stones anchored in the sand of your desert bioscape can give a balanced, Zen-like appearance to the terrarium. By selecting the most attractive, unique, or specially colored/shaped stones, you can claim a certain degree of artistic license in the construction of your terrarium.

But just as is true of substrates, not all types of rocks are suited to all styles of naturalistic terrarium. Actually, quite the opposite is true—most rock types only function properly when maintained within fairly strict environmental conditions. If put under environmental conditions in which it would not naturally occur, a rock or stone can react with its environment in any number of negative ways. If you know which types of rock to employ and which types not to employ in each style of terrarium, you'll find that rocks and stones make excellent, multipurpose additions to virtually any naturalistic terrarium.

Rocks to Avoid

The first and most important consideration before adding any rocks to your naturalistic terrarium is the health and welfare of your reptiles or amphibians. Many types of rock can be detrimental to your captive herps, and it's important that those varieties be identified and eliminated. Chalky, flaky, or easily crumbled stones are only very loosely bonded together, and they will break down quickly in moist or wet environments, such as jungles, swamps, bogs, or montane habitats. When they break down or dissolve, the stones will release chemical compounds that

Rockyards are sure to have interesting and suitable rocks for your terrarium, so if you have one locally be sure to check it out.

Shells and Bones

While many hobbyists enjoy the presence of sea shells or bones in their terrarium, adding these items is rarely a good idea. Sea shells, antlers, skulls, horns, and other similar organic materials will soon prove problematic in virtually any style of terrarium that is even somewhat moist. Sea shells, which simply don't look natural in anything except the marine fish tank, will rapidly break down into their calcium and carbon components, both of which will raise the pH of the terrarium into unacceptably alkaline levels.

In the presence of humidity, bone, antlers, and horns also will begin to deteriorate. Because of its extremely porous nature, rotting bone harbors millions of bacteria, fungi, spores, and other microorganisms that are harmful to your tank. Rotting bone is also a source of foul odor, and as more fungi grow, the bone will become discolored and unsightly. Perhaps the only instance in which bones could be successfully employed would be in the arid desert habitat, which would keep the skull or bone very dry and prevent it from hosting colonies of fungi and bacteria. Similarly, you could use small sea shells in a specialized habitat designed for marine crabs or hermit crabs.

will be soaked up by the terrarium environment. These alkaline agents can seriously pollute the enclosed quarters of your terrarium, killing the root systems of your plants and causing blood toxicity in many species of amphibians or skin complications in some reptiles. Toxic soils and water that have been polluted by decomposing stones often have to be disposed of, because cleaning the dissolved minerals from them is virtually impossible. For this reason, chalks, limestones, soap stones, micas, and similar types of rocks should never be used in naturalistic terrariums in which the relative humidity rises above 70 percent. Similarly, these stones should never be used in tanks in which they will be submerged in water or anchored in even mildly damp substrate.

Avoid oceanic rocks such as corals and calcium carbonates. When exposed to freshwater, these rocks break down very quickly, and they drive the alkalinity of the terrarium up. Herps such as frogs, toads, tadpoles, salamanders, and newts can all suffer severely if the stones you introduce to their environment radically alter the chemical composition of the soil and water in which they live and hunt. Stones that have a metallic sheen to them also may present problems, and some rocks will add copious amounts of sodium into your terrarium as they decompose, something you'll want to avoid.

Avoid rocks that contain brightly colored bands or streaks of red, green, blue, or yellow. Bright to dark red, powdery veins running through a rock indicate the presence of iron, which will rust in a moist tank. Dark green to light blue lines or streaks indicate that elemental copper is present in the stone. As the copper oxidizes, it can seriously pollute the soil and water of a terrarium, thereby posing a health risk to both the animal and plant inhabitants of the tank. Yellow veins in a rock may suggest the presence of sulfur, which will lead to unwanted difficulties in the terrarium's chemistry.

Rocks to Use

The best rocks to use are dense igneous or metamorphic forms that do not crumble or break apart under your grip. Darkly colored (various shades of gray) stones are typically acceptable, as are smooth, hard stones. Quartz crystals, which can be pink, white, red, gray, and deep purple, can add a vivid splash of color to any naturalistic terrarium, although they do not look natural in most habitats. Igneous and metamorphic rocks are your best bet, while sedimentary rocks (those that have a definite layered look to them) tend to contain most of the elements and minerals that you don't want in your terrarium.

If you are unsure as to which rocks are safe to use in your terrarium and which ones are not, ask an expert at the local rock yard or quarry, or contact the geology department of a university. You might be surprised at how accurately and thoroughly a college professor of geology will answer your rock-related questions.

Limestone and similar stones should only be used in dry terrariums, such as one housing collared lizards.

Some of the rules change, however, when you're adding rocks to the desert or savanna terrarium. Because these environments are perpetually dry and arid, chalky, flaky, and loosely constructed rocks will not decompose to pollute the habitat. Sandstone, limestone, and other such rocks may safely be employed in the desert vivarium. However, you should vary your stones considerably, even in the desert habitat. Simply because limestone and other easily degraded varieties can be used doesn't mean that they are the only stones that *should* be used. The rules regarding metallic luster and bright veins of coloration in rocks do not change for the desert environment; stones with bright veins of color *must not* be used in any captive environment.

Placement of Rocks

Once you've decided which rocks are safe for use in your chosen style of terrarium, the next phase of construction comes into play: placement. While the placement of stones and rocks within your terrarium may sound simple, it is actually quite important to understand exactly how the arrangement of these items can affect the plants and animals within the terrarium. Most stones and rocks should rest on the bottom and be anchored snugly within your substrate so that movement is not likely. Do not stand a tall stone upright in your terrarium and assume that it will stay that way for long. A slight bump or jar to the terrarium could cause the heavy stone to topple and fall.

Every year I hear of accidents in the naturalistic terrarium stemming from improperly placed stones. A falling rock may strike and crack (or shatter) the glass wall of the tank, or in an even worse scenario, the stone may fall atop your pet herp, injuring or even killing it. I learned about the dangers of falling rocks ten years ago. I had just incubated and hatched out a clutch of eastern kingsnake (*Lampropeltis getula getula*) eggs, and I kept the most beautiful hatchling of the clutch. A perfectly black specimen, this aberrantly colored animal lacked all traces of the white and yellow rings that earn this species the common name chain kingsnake. I had constructed a woodland habitat for my new pride and joy, and in it I placed a heavy slab of slate atop which my little snake could bask. Within 24 hours of constructing that habitat, the poorly anchored bit of slate shifted and fell, pinning the kingsnake hatchling to the floor of the tank. By the time I

If you house herps that bask heavily, such as uromastyx, position rocks under a heat lamp to provide a nice warm basking site.

found it, the snake had already expired. An engineering miscalculation cost a beautiful little reptile its life and cost me a one-of-a-kind pet.

Make sure that any large stones you use in your terrarium are seated firmly in the substrate and have no chance of shifting and falling. Of course, the phrase "seated firmly" is deceptively complex here; we are not talking about the same size or shape of stone, nor are we talking about the same eco-habitat for each keeper. And when we factor in the variable species that each hobbyist may keep, the issue becomes even more complicated. For example, a colony of green anoles (*Anolis carolinensis*) scampering over a large hunk of schist stone in a woodland terrarium isn't very likely to cause the rock to move. If, however, you place a pair of adult gopher tortoises (*Gopherus polyphemus*), which are powerful and accomplished burrowers, in the same environment, it would not be long before the tortoises' movement caused the heavy stone to shift and move any number of times before eventually settling to the bottom of the terrarium.

The bottom line is that you must know your environment, and you must know the habits of your pet herps to adequately anchor heavy stones within the terrarium. Rocks aren't likely to shift or fall if seated in dense substrate, but they are very likely to shift if anchored in loose substrates such as silica sands. Similarly, small, relatively weak herps or inverts are not likely to cause heavy stones to shift, while larger, stronger herps (tortoises, monitor lizards, crocodilians, pythons, and boas) are more likely to cause some items to shift. Burrowing species are particularly at risk of being

Raising pH

If you're constructing a swamp- or bog-style terrarium and the acidity of your substrate is too high to adequately support your desired species of plant life, you can use the chemical properties of some types of stone to help alleviate the problem. Limestone and some sandstones are highly alkaline. As these rocks break down in your swamp terrarium, they will help to raise the pH to levels that will accommodate plant growth. Placing several small hunks of limestone at various locations around your terrarium (especially those areas in which your plants are anchored) will help to maintain acceptable pH throughout the entire tank. If you have a large pool of water in the terrarium, place a few limestones in there in such a way that the current generated by your filter will force a continuous current of water directly over the small stones. This will increase the rate at which the stones decompose and disperse their pH-raising molecules throughout the terrarium.

You must be especially careful when placing rocks if you house strong, active, or burrowing herps—such as ridge-tailed monitors—in your terrarium.

injured by shifting or falling rocks, and their naturally subterranean habits can easily undermine the stability of the rock within the terrarium substrate. If you plan to house any form of burrowing herp, seat any and all large stones on the bottom of the terrarium, then add the substrate around it. This ensures that the herp can never burrow any lower than the very bottom of the stone, thus protecting it against the dangers of a shifting or moving stone.

Rock Hiding Places

A second matter of placement also concerns the shifting and sliding of rocks. While the commercial pet trade boasts of literally hundreds of varieties of hides and shelters, few of them are as visually pleasing or as ecologically correct as natural stone hiding places. In fact, most hides that are constructed out of black or tan plastic look out of place in the naturalistic terrarium, even if they are molded to resemble caves or other "natural" fixtures. The good news is that perfectly natural rocks and stones can be employed to construct interesting (and intricate) hides and shelters for your herps that will look perfectly natural and won't detract from the beauty and wild appearance of your naturalistic terrarium.

The best rocky hides are those that are only one piece, such as a naturally concave-shaped bit of Mexican lava rock. Once these items are firmly seated atop the substrate, there is very little to worry about as far as shifting and falling are concerned. But many hobbyists choose to construct hides or natural-looking caves out of multiple rocks or stones. Creating a shelter by layering flat or broad stones atop other stones is very dangerous. While this stone structure may be visually pleasing and may stand seemingly stable for months, the hobbyist is foolishly placing the health and safety of his reptile or amphibian at risk. Even a slight bump or jar to the terrarium could cause the stacked rocks to slide or shift and crush your beloved pet beneath them. And once the damage is done, it can't be undone. It's

Most desert- and savanna-dwelling reptiles will appreciate a rocky cave to hide in. A gray-banded kingsnake is shown here.

simply not worth the risk of injury to stack stones inside your terrarium. No matter how stable the rocks seem, the danger is always there. Fortunately, a number of tried and true methods of cave construction are available that are much safer and longer lasting than stacking.

Constructing Rock Caves The first method of cave construction calls for several pieces of igneous rock and twice as many black nylon zip-ties (also called cable ties, rat belts, and tie wraps). Igneous rock is better than both sedimentary and metamorphic types because they tend to crumble or break. Some of the hardest metamorphic and sedimentary rock that you can find also may work for this type of cave construction. Begin construction of the cave by placing all the rocks you plan to use on a table or workbench. Stack the rocks up in a cave-like formation to get a good idea of how you want them to look in your terrarium.

Once you have found the configuration that best suits your desires, make at least two (preferably three) strike marks on both stones at their seams with a piece of chalk so that each mark will align only when both stones are again stacked in that exact configuration. For example, after you've made three marks along the top and right-hand side of the cave, and then you remove the top, the marks will only align once more when the top of the cave is placed back on the rest of the rocks in exactly the same position. Once you've made all your marks, begin drilling small holes near each mark on each stone. Drill one hole for each mark. I suggest drilling with a metal-boring drill bit, or if you have access to it, drill with a stone-boring bit, although these bits can be fairly expensive. Once you've drilled all the holes in each rock, restack them so that all the strike marks align once more.

Run one end of the zip-tie through the hole in one rock, then run it through the corresponding (aligned) hole in the other rock, lace the end of the zip-tie back through its head, and pull tightly. You'll notice that the more you pull, the more tightly the zip-tie cinches down. Cinch as tightly as you can without cracking the rocks. Repeat until all the rocks have been securely bound by zip-ties. Use scissors or a sharp knife to clip off the excess tail of each zip-tie. You have just built a stable, sturdy, and long-lasting naturalistic cave that has virtually no chance of collapse.

One of the best aspects of this zip-tie cavern is that if you decide to reconfigure the cave, or if you wish to separate the rocks of the cave and employ them in some other fashion within your naturalistic terrarium, you need only remove the cave, cut through each zip-tie with a pair of scissors, and your rocks will instantly come apart. Stones bound in this manner can be used time and time again.

Another method of cavern building begins in the same manner: Gather all the stones you plan to use and place them on a table or workbench. Stack your stones and mark them with chalk to keep them aligned. Using a nontoxic epoxy resin, PVC cement, silicon, or Instacrete (a concrete bonding chemical), begin sealing the stones together. There is a wide variety of bonding products that will work for this purpose, but there is also a host of products that can pollute your terrarium, so read the warning labels on each product before beginning to make sure that your chosen sealant is suitable for indoor use. Once you've decided on the bonding agent that will work for you, start the process by smearing a liberal amount of sealant on the back edge of the right or left wall of the cave. Attach it to the edge of the back wall so that when they come together, the two stones will roughly form a right angle. Use a vise or some wooden chocks to hold the rocks in place until the sealant dries (usually 12 to 24 hours). Add the rest of your walls and the top stone of the cave in the same fashion. After the sealant dries, add any extra stones that you envision as part of your final cave structure.

Once all the stones are in place and the sealant has dried, you'll need to place the constructed cave in a sheltered outside environment, such as an open-air garage or on a porch. The airflow blowing through the porch or garage will help the sealant to further dry, and it will help to disperse the heavy, chemical odors emanating from the sealing agent. Make sure that no rain, snow, or other precipitation settles on the cave during this time. After 48 hours or so, bring the cave indoors and rinse it thoroughly in a bucket of water. Rinse several times. Once the sealant is dried, rinsed, and odor free, you may place it in your naturalistic terrarium. The only real drawback to this style of cavern is the permanence of the structure; once the glue or sealant sets, the stones are locked together forever.

If you only keep one or two small herps in your terrarium, then a basic, four-sided cave will normally suffice. But as your collection grows, you may want to experiment with larger and more elaborate designs. If you build a two- or even three-level structure (which will be very large and heavy, no matter what type of stone you employ), you should use a dualistic approach to the cavern's construction. If you use just the zip-tie method for such a large structure, the entire thing risks tilting and collapsing under its own weight—each zip-tie has just enough give to allow a heavy structure to buckle or fold, perhaps maiming or killing your pet in the process. If built purely by the bonding method, the heavy structure may work well for a long time before one of the lower joints suddenly gives, the sealant snapping under the tremendous weight and the entire cave shifting or collapsing.

Using both the zip-tie method in conjunction with the sealant-bonding method will grant your structure all the support it needs; if the sealant breaks or cracks, the zip-tie will prevent the mammoth cave from collapsing. I have only ever built a couple of these cavern "super structures" for use in the naturalistic terrarium, but when you put the time and effort into making one the proper way, it can be a thing of beauty. Colonies of leopard geckos, African fat-tailed geckos, and desert horned lizards love to climb upon and explore these rocky structures.

Other Rocky Features

The beauties of rock structures do not end with the construction of the cavern hideaway—not by a long shot.

Rocky Mounds Rocky outcroppings, or "mounds"—meaning, in this case, a jumbled pile of stones—can be just as impressive as a cavern. Simply arrange your stones in a configuration in which they are naturally stable and cement them together, just as you would for the cavern structure. (Hint: If you stack the stones on a flat table and they do not fall with a little jostling, that's a naturally stable configuration.) A large rock mound can be

Rocky mounds and walls can provide your herps with a vertical temperature gradient, exemplified in this desert terrarium housing collared lizards.

placed in the center of your terrarium as a centralized gathering place for a colony of basking herps, such as fence lizards, agamas, or uromastyx. A smattering of smaller rock mounds can be placed at various locations throughout a terrarium to serve as natural structures.

Rock mounds can be especially useful when it comes to basking herps. When a snake or lizard wakes in the morning, it typically moves out of hiding and into a bright, sunny area to soak up the sun's warmth. After its body temperature is sufficiently warm, the reptile moves off to hunt or seek a mate. If a herp's body temperature gets too warm, it only needs to seek a shady spot to cool down. Basking in the wild is very easy for herps to do, but in captivity, it can be much more difficult. In many instances, the terrarium is kept too cool, so the herps living there may never attain their preferred bodily temperatures. Conversely, many hobbyists keep their pets' habitat too hot, so the animals may suffer or even die when unable to escape the heat. In the home terrarium, therefore, it is necessary to establish a vertical thermocline situated directly beneath the heating apparatus of the terrarium.

Placing a flat stone directly beneath your terrarium's heating lamp will provide a basking spot, but it may not get your herp as close to the light/heat as it needs to be. By building a rock mound (again, using nontoxic sealant to secure the mound) that extends to about one-third to one-half the way up the tank, you can create a vertical range of basking territory for your herp, and then it's up to the reptile to choose the level at which it wants to bask.

Rocky Pools Another commonly encountered and very popular form of stone structure is the rocky pool or swimming bowl. Constructed using a large chunk of Mexican lava rock, this structure can add a very unique dimension to virtually any style of naturalistic terrarium. Begin by selecting an appropriately sized piece of Mexican lava, a rock renowned by hobbyists for its naturally concave, bowl-like formation. Find a piece that has as wide and deep a bowl to it as you possibly can. Place the lava rock on a table or workbench and spread a thin layer of nontoxic sealing agent (the same type used to secure the walls of your cavern will work) inside the entire bowl with a paintbrush or foam spreader, both of which are available in the paint section of any hardware store. Get a layer of sealant inside every little nook and cranny inside the bowl. Allow it to dry for 48 to 72 hours. Then, move the bowl outside to allow it to air out.

After it is thoroughly dry, fill the bowl portion of the rock with water and let it sit. Monitor it for any leaks. If leaks occur, repeat the sealing/drying process. If there are no leaks, wash the bowl out with clean water about a half-dozen times to rid the bowl of any loose bits of sealant.

Now you're ready to anchor your perfectly natural-looking stone bowl in your terrarium. If used in a desert- or savanna-style terrarium, this structure makes an excellent water dish for snakes and large lizards. And if you employ a large, deep stone bowl in a jungle- or woodland-style terrarium, it can double as a spawning pool for various frog and toad species.

Rocky Arches

One of the most impressive rock structures I've ever seen was built by a friend of mine back in the 1980s. She built a tall stone arch, just like those that form naturally in Utah and Arizona, in a 200-gallon (757-l) desert terrarium dedicated to various species of horned lizards. By carefully choosing her stones (she used red shale) and patiently adhering them together with the proper bonding agent, she completed her very natural-looking archway in about a month. After the initial arch was finished, my friend carefully sanded the solid structure, which measured some 40 inches long by 22 inches high (102 x 56 cm) at its apex, to eliminate the lines between the stones. When it was all said and done, it looked from a distance to be a natural arch formed from one piece of stone. Her lizard colony scaled and basked upon the arch almost constantly, and her friends were sick with envy that she'd built such a unique and impressive structure.

Rock Garden

Often, hobbyists think that plants only thrive in soil, but this is not always the case. A wide variety of mosses, algae, and other primitive plants thrive directly on the exposed face of a rock. Given a constant supply of ample moisture, these plants, which are not adversely affected by the high mineral content of granite-based rocks, will grow in your terrarium the same way they would grow in nature. Primitive plants, such as mosses, and plant-like organisms, such as lichens and algae, lack roots and vascular systems, so they do not need soil. Because of this lack of vesicles and roots, however, such plants also require a constant supply of moisture, such as from a pool, spray from a waterfall, or frequent fogs.

Bear in mind that temperate mosses need a winter cooling period if they are to survive, so your best bet is to use tropical specimens, such as those available from specialty online retailers or through local pet shops, instead of harvesting mosses from the wild. Algae, however, need no such cooling period. Lichens are often tough to keep alive in the home terrarium because of their exacting temperature, moisture, and lighting needs.

As well-known herpetologist and writer Rex Lee Searcey once wrote, some reptile species are "water incompetent," and if they were to fall into a deep or steep-sided water dish, these animals might drown before they could escape the dish. Small, land-dwelling turtles and tortoises are particularly prone to such accidents. Always take great care when providing watering dishes to your herps. Only provide dishes that those animals can climb out of if they accidentally fall inside.

Drainage Layer

Of course, not all functional stones need to be seen in the terrarium. Some subsurface rocks can make a world of difference in your terrarium, even though they may never see the light of day. In a great many ecosystems, stones and rocks occur just a few feet (meters) beneath the organic soil. These rocks serve not only to provide solid, stable anchoring points for the roots of large plants and trees, but they also allow excess water to drain away from the roots of all plants. If the root systems of most plant species (excluding swamp-dwelling or aquatic species) stay totally immersed in water, they will soon canker and rot, the beneficial fungi (mycorrhizae) that transfer nutrients from the soil into the root hairs essentially drowning. With the roots rotting and no source of nutrient intake, the plant will quickly wither and die. But as the water drains away from the roots through the gaps and crevasses between the rocks, the plant draws ample moisture from the semi-damp soil, the mycorrhizae will continue to function normally, and the ecosystem will continue to thrive.

Coarse gravel makes the best drainage layer in most cases. It is readily available at most pet stores.

This principle of water drainage holds true in the home terrarium as well. As your plants mature and send their roots deeper and deeper into the substrate mix, their roots will eventually grow down to the bottom of the tank. If the nutrient-rich substrate at the bottom of the tank stays perpetually wet, any roots that are growing that deep will begin to canker and die back. Once decay sets into the root, it can easily spread up through the root system and destroy the entire plant. Prevent this from happening by placing at least 2 inches (5 cm) of aquarium pea gravel in the bottom of the terrarium before adding any substrate mix. As you water your terrarium, any excess water will drain down through the soil and disperse amid the layer of pea gravel. As your plants mature and their roots snake deeper into the substrate and eventually into the pea-gravel layer, small bits and pieces of their roots may die off or "drown" in any water contained within the gravel. This is okay, because even though the tips of these roots may perish, the bulk of the root system will be safely anchored in the nutrient-rich substrate located *above* the drainage zone, and your plant will thrive.

Maintaining a drainage layer of pea gravel is also critical to the successful propagation of the beneficial bacteria and fungi that you want to thrive within your substrate mixture. Simply stated, these micro good guys cannot survive if they are kept overly wet or are completely submerged under water. As the water in your terrarium drains down into the gravel, the substrate mix will absorb whatever amount of water it needs and no more. This ensures that the fungi can flourish, the decomposers can feed on animal waste, and all the necessary chemical and biological processes that need to occur in your terrarium will transpire unimpeded by perpetual wetness.

A word of warning is in order, however, because not all small pebble-like stones are suitable for use as a drainage layer within the terrarium. As you've already learned, certain types of rocks decompose more quickly than others, and some have more alkaline (basic) properties than others. It would be unwise, therefore, to deposit a layer of limestone or some other sodium- and calcium-rich stone as your drainage layer, because such stones would very quickly throw off the pH balance of your substrate mix and hinder proper plant growth. Similarly, no organic materials should be used, such as crushed coral, because the same scenario of decomposition and leaching would occur. Perhaps even more undesirable than that is the fact that if the drainage materials break down, the gaps between these items will vanish, and the drainage layer will cease to exist. Another type of stone to avoid is anything that has been chemically coated or altered in any way. Many types of gravel meant for decorative purposes have been coated in clear resin, painted, dyed, or otherwise dipped in some type of chemical. Adding such stones to your terrarium can result in the contamination of the substrate mix, and depending on just what type of chemical the stones have on them, perhaps even the

Note the drainage layer of small stones in this small woodland terrarium housing a rose-haired tarantula. Almost all natural terrariums will benefit from a drainage layer.

Natural Terrariums

death of your plants as well. Fortunately, it is easy to recognize chemically treated stones. Brightly colored stones (such as hot pinks, purples, yellows, reds, and blues) do not occur naturally, so any stone that bears such wild coloration has certainly been painted or dyed and has no place within the naturalistic terrarium. Stones that have been coated in clear resin will appear very shiny, glossy, or even have a perpetually "wet" look to them.

The best type of stone to use in constructing a drainage layer is the simple earth-toned, rounded, pea-sized pebble. These stones have been harvested from riverbeds and have a nearly neutral pH. They are tough, smooth, inert, and highly resistant to erosion or decomposition. These stones are widely available at hardware stores and nurseries and are very inexpensive; pea gravel will be one of the cheapest items you add to your naturalistic terrarium. Prepare these stones by thoroughly rinsing them in cold water to wash away any debris and silt before constructing the drainage layer inside your terrarium. Many hobbyists have discovered that a bucket with a series of small holes (smaller than the pebbles) drilled in the bottom works very well for this task; simply empty the bag of pebbles into the bucket and hose down the stones. The silt and sand debris will wash away through the holes in the bottom of the bucket.

Separating the Layers

Some experts suggest that, as your substrate mixture matures and settles within your terrarium, small bits of this substrate will sink down and gradually fill in the gaps and nooks within your drainage layer through which excess water drains away from the rest of the substrate. When this happens, the substrate layer and the drainage layer will essentially become one, and your terrarium will lose the benefits of even having a drainage layer. Prevent this problem from occurring by laying a sheet of household or industrial air conditioner filter atop your drainage layer of pea gravel before you lay down your substrate layer. This fine-mesh filter will prevent any solid particles from your substrate layer from slipping down into your pea-gravel drainage layer, but it will still allow ample water drainage. A plastic fiber air conditioner filter easily can be cut to fit most terrariums, and because it is virtually indestructible, it will last in your terrarium for years to come.

Chapter 5

Adding & Maintaining Plants

Aside from your pet herps or invertebrates, your plants are the most intricate and interesting forms of life in your vivarium. How can plants be interesting, you ask? They are slow-growing life forms that gradually change and mature over time. In the comings and goings of our day-to-day lives, we may not notice the extra flush of growth that comes upon the cypress trees in our backyards or the additional 6 inches (15 cm) of tendril that has grown on the stand of English ivy by our front doors. With our busy schedules of work, school, parenting, and other tasks, we all too often overlook the "smaller" things in life, like plant growth.

The inclusion of live plants may be the defining characteristic of the natural terrarium. This tropical forest terrarium includes roughly a half-dozen species of plants and a ball python.

When your plants are growing and thriving *inside* the captive terrarium, they come under a far greater degree of scrutiny: The hobbyist arrives home and checks daily the height, color, rigidity, and health of his plants. Are they too moist? Too dry? Too cold? Too hot? Did I add enough fertilizer? When do I need to trim them back? These questions and others seem to push their way into the forefront of the hobbyist's mind, and with good reason. Every inch (cm) that your plants grow, every new leaf they add to their foliage, and every petal on every bloom are living, growing signs that you are doing an excellent job of maintaining and sustaining your naturalistic terrarium.

The Plant Community

The first and perhaps most vital consideration that hobbyists must embrace is the plant community, with "community" referring to the plants that would naturally thrive in the wild ecosystem that you choose to mimic within your terrarium. For example, if you begin to construct a jungle-style terrarium (warm temperature, high humidity, slightly acidic soil, moderate to intense lighting, etc.), you can only expect to have success with plants that naturally thrive under those circumstances—plants that grow best within that plant community. Your jungle terrarium must, therefore, comprise bromeliads, ferns, broad-leafed tropicals, and other such plants. Should you choose to add arid-loving varieties, such as cacti, aloe, or other succulents, the high humidity of the jungle terrarium will liquefy those water-retaining species. Conversely, if you are constructing a savanna or desert terrarium, you cannot trick yourself into thinking that the dainty fronds and thin trunk of a silk oak could survive there. You must resign yourself to the fact that cacti and succulents, such as *Haworthia* or *Gasteria*, are your preferred options.

Select plants based on their adaptations to the land/soil, pH, temperature, moisture (in ground), airborne humidity, light intensity, and other such physical parameters of the wild habitats from which they come. If the plants you choose are not naturally adapted to the bioscape you have created, the outcome will be unsuccessful. I've seen many hobbyists run into one frustrating roadblock after another because they attempted to mix species of plants that do not thrive under the same environmental conditions—species that are not part of the same plant community.

Mix desert plants with desert plants and jungle plants with jungle plants. The only areas of overlap when selecting plants occur when two or more habitats share common features that will allow plants from multiple communities to thrive. A warm, moist swamp environment could, for example, accommodate a selection of plants that would normally only thrive in the jungle environment.

Plant Scientific and Common Names

Like other forms of life, plants have both scientific and common names. However, many common plants are actually referred to by their scientific names at least as frequently as they are by their common names. For example, a snake plant is as likely to be called *Sansevieria* as it is snake plant. The name is italicized whether it is used as a common or scientific name for the sake of consistency.

In addition to the normal common and scientific names, some plants have "cultivars." These are forms of a plant species produced through selective crossings and possibly hybridization. A cultivar is put in single quotation marks after the scientific name, e.g., *Sansevieria* 'Moonshine.'

Available Species and Cultivars

This is not a horticultural book, nor is the material that is about to follow in any way definitive or complete. As with all aspects of terrarium construction and maintenance, the sky's the limit when it comes to the finer details. The plants that appeal to one hobbyist may not appeal to another, or the method of watering that one hobbyist prefers may not work in your specific terrarium. This is okay because there is such a wide variety of plant species available that the individual differences disappear beneath an ocean of successful variation. With that in mind, here are some plants that can thrive in one type naturalistic terrarium or another.

Desert Terrarium Plants

These rugged, hardy, and succulent plants have adapted over the eons for life in one of the earth's harshest environments. Capable of withstanding prolonged periods of draught, these plants will suffer under conditions that would seem ideal for woodland or jungle plants; too much water or relative humidity can spell doom for these species. Desert plants are defined by their need for bright light, high temperatures, low humidity, and seasonal dormant periods (from October to March for many species). For best results, do not add much water at all to your desert plants during this period, and increase the amount of lighting they receive.

Cacti encompass a wide family of plants that occurs in virtually all the deserts of North and South America. They appear in many forms, from the oval and ball-shaped variety to the tall slender types to the spade-shaped "bunny ear" varieties. And the prickly spines for which cacti are famous also range from thick, woody spines to fine hair- or fur-like wisps adorning the cactus' stalk. (This is especially prevalent in species in the genera *Cephalocereus* and *Espostoa*). The type of cacti you choose to keep in your terrarium will depend on the species of herps or invertebrates you house. Thick-scaled, robust species can be housed with thick-spine varieties, while invertebrates fare best with hairy or woolly cacti. Most cacti have high light requirements, so be sure that you can accommodate the lighting needs of your chosen species. Some of the most popular cacti varieties are described in the sidebar located within this chapter.

The snake plants (*Sansevieria*) are hardy and attractive plants for dry terrariums. There are literally hundreds of varieties available.

Of course, cacti aren't the only species to make excellent specimens in the desert vivarium. Other species thrive and flourish in

Poisonous Plants

The following is a list of commonly available poisonous plants that may pose a serious health threat to any herbivorous or omnivorous species if ingested. Do not include these plants in any terrarium housing herps that eat plants.

Amaryllis	Cyclamen	Jimson Weed	Pokeweed
Anemone	Daffodil	Larkspur	Privet
Azalea	Dieffenbachia	Lily of the Valley	Rhododendron
Belladonna	English Ivy	Milkweed	Rhubarb
Bird of Paradise	Foxglove	Mistletoe	Sage
Bottlebrush	Hemlock	Morning Glory	Snapdragon
Buttercup	Holly	Oleander	Tulip
Calla Lily	Hyacinth	Pennyroyal	Verbena
Christmas Cactus	Impatiens	Philodendron	Wisteria
Crocus	Iris	Poinsettia	Yew
Croton	Jasmine	Poison Ivy/Oak	Yucca

arid environments as well. The first of these genera are the *Sansevieria*, or the snake plants. *Sansevieria* plants are highly variable, with blade-like leaves or sculptural leaves and stems, and they grow under a wide range of arid conditions. A favorite of desert vivarium keepers, these plants fare best in bright, indirect light, so do not place them directly under spotlights or bright UV bulbs. They require well-drained soil or their roots and bases will mold and rot. Popular cultivars include 'Gray Lady,' 'Moonshine,' 'Bantel's Sensation,' 'Golden Hahnii,' and 'Fan Form.'

The genus *Euphorbia* also offers a wide variety of unique plants for the desert terrarium. Many cultivars of these twisted-stemmed, wrinkled-leafed plants fare well in the captive environment, but there are certain rules that apply to their keeping. Because all varieties of *Euphorbia* contain a resinous sap of irritating latex that can prove caustic to the skin of animals that break a plant, or even noxious or lethal to herbivorous animals that eat some of the plant, these species only should be kept around small, carnivorous species. Most species of *Euphorbia* require intense levels of lighting. Because these plants have a large following, they are widely cultivated, and many online retailers will ship cultivars of *Euphorbia* to your door for minimal expense.

Commonly Available Cactus

Name	Height (inch/cm)	Flowers?	Description
Aporocactus flagelliformus Rat's Tail Cactus	24/6	Yes	A long, low-growing species, this cactus does best in wide, broad environments with indirect, bright lighting.
Astrophytum capricorn Goat's Horn	8/20	Yes	Bulbous and low when young, but growing taller with age, this species bears long, irregular grey spines. Needs full light.
Chamaecereus silvestrii Peanut Cactus	18/46	Yes	A fast growing, rapidly spreading variety that grows along the ground in peanut-shaped shoots. Flowers prolifically.
Cleistocactus straussii Silver Torch	36/91	Yes	Bears fine thorns. Requires full light and grows easily under novice care.
Echinocactus grusonii Barrel Cactus	24/61	No	Very slow growing. Does best in semi-shaded areas.
Echinocereus knippelianus Knippel's Cactus	4/10	Yes	A very small, knobby cactus that is also fast growing. Small spines. Fares best in moderate light.
Echinopsis eyriesii Sea Urchin Cactus	6/15	Yes	A squat species with thick, sharp spine-clusters. Flowers are very tall.
Ferocactus latispinus Fish Hook Cactus	16/41	Yes	Slow-growing but easily kept species. Spines range in color from reddish brown to deep purple. Semi-direct light.
Gymnocalycium mihanovichii Hibotan Cactus	3/8	Yes	Squat and vibrantly colored yellow to pink or red. Frequently seen grafted atop a basal stalk of *Hylocereus*. Half-shade.
Notocactus leninghausii Golden Ball	36/91	Yes	Tall species, but very slow growing. Thick stalk with very fine, hair-like spines. Flowers are yellow.
Oputina microdasys Bunny Ears	24/61	Yes	Pads are thick, and growth is fast and prolific. Full-light.
Parodia sanguiniflora Tom Thumb Cactus	10/25	Yes	A slow growing, squatty, bulbous cactus. Popular and easily cultivated.
Rebitua miniscula Mexican Sunball	3/8	Yes	Grows in tight clumps; bears bright red flowers in spring. Semi-shade.
Trichocereus grandiflorus Torch Cactus	14/36	Yes	Stalk is thicker at top than at base. Flowers in spring. Spines thin but rigid. Prefers semi-shade. Commonly Available Cacti

Other excellent plants for the desert terrarium include those hailing from the genera *Aloe, Haworthia,* and *Gasteria.* Known far and wide for their medicinal properties, *Aloe* comes in a variety of species such as *A. variegate, A. jucunda, A. aristata, A. rauhii,* and *A. ciliaris.* Most aloe species need lots of light and a damp root system. (I prefer to anchor them using the in-pot method of planting.) Dwarf species rarely outgrow even small natural vivariums.

Species from the genus *Haworthia* also fare best when maintained in pots, rather than in the soil matrix of the terrarium. Because the leaves and stems of these plants are easily damaged, only use them with small snakes and light-bodied lizards such as geckos or small skinks. Some of the more hardy and attractive species include *H. fasciata, H. browniana, H. maughanii, H. truncate,* and the slow-growing *H. margaritifera.*

Finally, the members of the *Gasteria* genus include some thick-leaved, slow-growing species commonly known as cow tongue or ox tongue. If the spines on the leaves of your *Gasteria* species become too sharp, trim them back with a pair of scissors or fingernail clippers. Some aloes also can have large spines on their leaves. All members of the *Aloe, Haworthia,* and *Gasteria* genera require intense levels of lighting.

Haworthia are excellent plants for the desert terrarium. Here are two commonly available species, the star window plant (*H. tessellata*) (top) and the pearl plant (*H. margaritafera*) (bottom).

Several species of the genus *Ficus* also work well in large desert terrariums. Also known as caudexed fig trees, *F. petiolaris* and *F. palmeri* are slow-growing, woody-stemmed leafy trees with a water-storing stem. Both work well in bright, arid terrariums. They do break easily under the weight of large reptiles such as monitors and boids, however. Avoid overwatering because an excess of moisture causes these plants to drop their leaves.

Woodland and Jungle Plants

The plants common to the woodland/jungle terrarium are some of the most versatile species in the hobby because they can tolerate the conditions of either the temperate woodland tank or the tropical jungle tank. Of course, not all species will thrive in either terrarium type, but by and large, most species can adapt to life in either terrarium type.

Broad-leafed and thick-stemmed, the forest plants need moist soil, but most cannot tolerate standing water around their root systems; a thick drainage layer, therefore, is in order. Most of the plants described in this section are also moderate- to low-light plants because their native jungle or forest conditions offer them sunlight that is filtered through the forest canopy above. (That's why many have big leaves, so that they may catch all available light in a heavily shaded environment.) When watered and fertilized regularly and offered suitable lighting, the plants detailed here should live and thrive in just about any woodland or jungle environment.

Some excellent plants that fit the bill of the woodland or jungle tank hail from the genera *Fatsia* and *Fittonia*. Native to the cool forests of Japan and Taiwan, the *Fatsia* species that are more commonly available include *F. japonica*, *F. oligocarpella*, and *F. polycarpa*. These are very broad-leafed species that do best when exposed to moderate lighting and temperatures that do not exceed 80° to 84° F (26.5° to 29°C). If used in a mixed-plant community, the *Fatsia* species, which can grow to several yards (meters) in height in time, will cast much shade on lower-growing species. It may require trimming.

Fittonia, on the other hand, is a much lower-growing plant that makes excellent ground cover for forest-floor herps, such as tiger salamanders and toads of all varieties. The most popular species, which is available through virtually any nursery or plant dealer, is *F. vershaffeltii*, which is commonly called the mosaic plant or nerve plant. The mosaic plant needs a light watering every few days; if allowed to dry out, the plant will wilt noticeably, but a good watering will perk it right back up again. Under superior conditions, the mosaic plant is a prolific grower. A chart in this chapter lists many other woodland plants that are most suitable for growing in a terrarium.

Wetland Plants

A final grouping of plants contains those that are suitable only for life in the swamp or wetland environment. As a general rule, swamp plants require a much higher level of light intensity than do woodland/jungle plants because life on the surface of a lake or in the reedy shallows of a pond affords considerable exposure to sunlight that is not filtered through a forest canopy.

Commonly Available Woodland Plants

Name	Height (inches/cm)	Description
Aglaonema commutatum 'White Rajah'	18/46	This cultivar of Chinese evergreen will thrive in deep shade; makes an excellent staple to virtually any woodland or jungle terrarium.
Asparagus declinatus Foxtail Fern	12/30	A finely built, yet sturdy fern, this species does best when the soil is kept slightly damp, yet allowed to drain fully. Moderate lighting.
Aspidistra elatior Cast Iron Plant	24/61	Deep green with long, oblong leaves, this plant is extremely hardy. Thrives in well drained soil and moderate to dim light conditions.
Asplenium nidus Bird's Nest Fern	15/38	A stalwart and easily cultivated fern that flourishes in less than ideal conditions. Soil must drain well, or roots will rot.
Chlorophytum comosum Spider Plant	12/30	A very prolific and hardy species. Requires moderate lighting and superior drainage. May require trimming to prevent hostile takeover of vivarium.
Costus sanguineus Spiral Flag	18/46	Fast growing and rugged plant; can be used with larger herps. Prefers an alkaline soil mixture with a small amount of powdered limestone added at to the substrate.
Dieffenbachia picta Dumb Cane	18/46	Grows well in low light conditions with moist, drained soil. Sap and leaves toxic.
Dracaena marginata Dragon's Tree	7 feet/2 m	Long, spear-shaped leaves rosette out from central stalk, which, in time, will mature into a woody trunk. Best kept in very large terrariums. *Dracaena* is a very diverse genus with something in it for every hobbyist's needs.
Hedera canariensis variegata Algerian Ivy	12/30	Easily the most desirable ivy for the terrarium; excellent ground cover and climbing vine. Requires moderate to bright light. Do not fertilize for 3-4 months after purchase and planting.
Philodendron cordatum Heart-Leaf Philodendron	12/30	A best-bet for beginning vivarium keepers. Prolific and fast growing, this plant adapts well to a wide variety of captive conditions. Drained soil and moderate lighting. A very forgiving specimen.
Schefflera actinophylla Umbrella Tree	3 feet/1 m or taller	A tall-growing tree with woody stems and large leaves; will require trimming or it will outgrow the terrarium. Requires 4 hours or more of bright light daily
Scindapsus aureus Pothos or Devil's Ivy	long vine	Low-growing or climbing vine that can reach many feet in length but can be kept pruned to fit the terrarium. Leaves are deep green in low light, or silvery/pale green in bright conditions.
Tolmiea menziesii Piggyback Plant	6-8/15-20	Low growing ground cover that reproduces readily in captivity. Fertilize every two months with a phosphorus-rich blend. Thrives in alkaline soil. Bright light.

Flowers in the Desert

If you have added one or more varieties of flowering cacti to your terrarium, you may become frustrated if your plant refuses to flower. Before you throw in the towel, here are a few pointers to remember:

- **Most cacti only flower once they have reached three to four years of age.**
- **About half the cactus species will bloom only after a period of "neglect." Care for (water and fertilize) your cacti through the spring and summer months, and offer them very little during the fall and winter months. The result should be a prolonged and prolific blooming period the following spring.**
- **Many cacti species seem more prone to flower when they are slightly pot-bound, so an in-pot planting may be in order rather than in-substrate planting.**
- **Bear in mind that cacti of the genera *Oputina* and *Cereus* can be reluctant to flower in captivity.**

The plants detailed in the accompanying chart are, of course, not exhaustive of the total variety of swamp plants available, nor are they exclusive of other plant species. For example, many woodland/jungle plants also may thrive in the well-drained, upland regions of a swamp terrarium.

Lucky bamboo (*Dracaena sanderiana*), which is often sold in novelty shops and is not closely related to true bamboos, can make a good wetland terrarium addition, although its roots are very sensitive to pH shifts (excessively alkaline conditions can be quickly fatal to the plant, while overly acidic conditions lead to a blanching of the leaves and a softening of the stalk) because it is a very fast-growing species that will require trimming. Arboreal tree frogs, however, may enjoy perching on the vertical stalks of a close-growing cluster of lucky bamboo.

A wide variety of fully aquatic and submersible plants are also viable options for the wetland terrarium that has deep enough pools to sustain them.

Terrarium Size and Shape

A second parameter that the hobbyist must weigh is the compatibility of the plants he selects with the physical dimensions of his terrarium. While moss or low, squatty cacti can be successfully housed in even the smallest of naturalistic terrariums, a wide variety of species may require an especially tall or wide terrarium in which to thrive. *Ficus* and *Schefflera* need plenty of vertical space in which to grow, as do many species of *Sanseveria* and palm. While these plants are anchored in the substrate and grow upward, many species should be

Fittonia are hardy plants for woodland and rainforest terrariums. They stay small, making good ground cover.

planted high in the tank (like from a hanging pot attached to the top of the terrarium), and that same need for vertical space comes into play as these plants grow downward toward the substrate. Examples of commonly used downward-reaching plants are burro's tail, philodendron, Canary Island ivy, and rosary vine. Tall plants, or those that require plenty of vertical space, will fare poorly in terrariums that are too short to accommodate their needs.

Width, or horizontal space, is also a major factor when planning the vegetative layout of your naturalistic terrarium. As much as you might like to place a dense cluster of bamboo closely beside a small grove of spider plants, this might not be a viable option. Both spider plant and bamboo have shallow running roots that extend horizontally through the soil. The result of planting them too close together would be fierce competition between the two plant species for nutrients, water, and space to expand; the roots of each species would, in time, choke out the other. You would be better off planting these two species very far apart so that each may expand as much as possible within the terrarium.

The matter of horizontal space also comes into play when you consider not only those parts of the plants that are underground but those parts that are above ground: the leaves and foliage. A hobbyist who adds a small Japanese *Fatsia* to a woodland terrarium may be unpleasantly surprised when that plant's leaves unfurl to their full width of 12 to 16 inches (12.5 to 40.6 cm) across. Any plants growing under the massive canopy of the *Fatsia* will begin to suffer quickly from light deficiency and will soon pale and wither for want of more illumination.

Conversely, some species of low-growing tropical plant may require heavily filtered lighting, such as is naturally weakened by a thick coverage of overhead jungle canopy and foliage. Such species would then require that they be planted directly under the foliage of a taller, more broad-leafed plant species, because if planted out in the open under direct lighting, these shade-loving species would suffer and never grow to their fullest, most lush potential. Getting the vertical and horizontal spacing issues in your naturalistic terrarium correct is vital to the welfare of each plant within the tank and also to the success of the terrarium as a whole.

Plant—Animal Compatibility

Once you've researched your desired plant species and picked out those that will thrive in your terrarium biome, you must consider how these plant species will fare in the company of your reptilian, amphibian, or invertebrate pets. More importantly, you'll need to consider how your pets will fare in the company of your plants, for to lose a plant because of a raucous or herbivorous herp is one thing, but to lose a herp due to a toxic or otherwise dangerous plant is quite another matter altogether.

Dangers to Plants

Plants may be trampled by heavy or powerful herps, or they may be eaten by herbivorous species. A cluster of dracaena growing along the edge of a water source in a jungle terrarium may come under attack by the hungry jaws of a green iguana, should it take an interest in nibbling on the plant's bright red and green leaves. As the iguana takes repeated snacks at the dracaena's expense, the once lush, thriving plant soon will be reduced to a brown and dying trunk projecting up from the soil. Similarly, within a month or so of being continually subjected to a Nile monitor's movements about the terrarium, a once-thriving stand of Fittonia will be badly tattered and trampled down.

Bird's-nest fern (*Asplenium nidus*) does well in moist soil, but it also grows 2-3 feet (60-90 cm) in height and has delicate leaves.

The solution to both of these scenarios is to replace the beleaguered plants with something that is far more compatible with the terrarium's reptilian inhabitants. In the case of the green iguana, a less-appetizing species of plant can be cultivated. Both the parlor palm and the butterfly palm grow well in the iguana's humid, tropical environment, and their thin, flavorless leaves rarely attract the appetites of any reptilian herbivores. In the terrarium hosting the Nile monitor, the *Fittonia* could easily be replaced by virtually any species of tropical or temperate ivy. Not only can ivy's thick tendrils and tough, waxy leaves withstand a considerable amount of trampling and foot-traffic by most of the moderately large herps, but its rapid growth and near-total ground coverage also make it especially resilient when cultivated in the same terrarium with a heavy-bodied reptile.

Keepers of chameleons and other arboreal herps frequently use *Ficus benjaminica* in their terrariums. Use *Ficus* with caution because they secrete an irritating sticky sap when injured.

Dangers to Animals

Of course, the opposite scenarios are also possible. For example, say that you are keeping and maintaining a swamp terrarium in which you are both simulating the natural swamps of the American South and maintaining a breeding colony of green anoles. If you choose to add both the pitcher plants into that terrarium, you've made a dangerous mistake, and your anoles just might pay for it with their lives. The northern pitcher plant (*Sarracenia purpurea*) has specially adapted leaves that grow into deep, cylindrical formations. The inner surfaces of these leaves are very slick and steep. Their dark recesses attract insects by emitting a sickly-sweet aroma, which is very similar to that of rotting meat. Once the insect ventures inside one of the columnar leaves, it loses footing on the inner surface and falls to the bottom, where it is dissolved by the plant's acidic saps and a community of microorganisms. The nutrients of the dissolved insect are then absorbed by the plant. Should one of your hatchling anoles wander inside the bowl of one of the pitcher plant's leaves, it would almost certainly be unable to escape and would perish inside the leaf.

Commonly Available Wetland Plants

Name	Height (inches/cm)	Description
Acorus calamus Sweet Flag	8/20	A tall, grass-like plant, the sweet flag requires nutrient rich soil under water. Best kept in very large vivaria. Bright light.
Alisma plantago aquatica Water Plantain	14/36	Tall, broad-leafed plant. Requires bright light and no more than 3 inches (8 cm) of water. Best kept in a tall tank.
Alternanthera philoxeroides Alligator Weed	4-6/10-15	Grows equally well in water or on land; this creeper provides excellent cover for shallow-dwelling herps. Highly invasive to many habitats, so dispose of cuttings carefully.
Carex comosa Bottlebrush Sedge	12/30	A shore-dwelling species, this easily kept plant adds dimension and ground cover to any tank. Toxic if consumed. Bright light.
Eichhornia crassipes Water Hyacinth	24/61	Floating. Stalks can grow to over two feet tall, and roots can form a thick, oxygen-starving blanket over the surface of the water. Must be trimmed regularly. Needs very bright light.
Hydrocotyle umbellata Pennywort	4/10	An excellent, hardy ground-cover for shorelines and pond edges. Needs bright light. Leaves shaped like an umbrella.
Ludwigia repens Red Ludwigia	10/25	Sporting green leaves on a red stem, this creeper grows on land and over open water. Very hardy in bright light.
Marsilea mutica Floating Water Clover	2/5	A floating species of fern, that reproduces via spores, this plant is easily grown in bright light. Fertilize sparingly.
Phyla lanceolata Frog Fruit	2/5	Ideal ground cover for any terrarium, this plant needs moderately bright light. Fragrant and fast growing, frog fruit may need regular trimming.
Pistia stratiotes Water Lettuce	3/8	A floating, broad leafed plant with long, trailing roots. Excellent at filtering water column and providing cover for aquatic herps. Need very bright light.
Sagittaria graminea Arrowhead	18/46	A thin-stemmed, broad leafed species, this is a hardy and popular plant. Dwarf cultivars, such as 'Bloom n Baby' do not exceed 10 inches (25 cm) in height. Prolific runner.
Spirodela polyrhiza Giant Duckweed	0.5/1	A tiny floating plant that, unchecked, can reproduce aggressively. Offers excellent cover for small aquatic herps. Requires very bright light.

While baby anoles in the wild might rarely be captured by a pitcher plant, remember that the naturalistic terrarium is only so large, and in such an enclosed environment, a baby anole will be in considerable danger around either of these carnivorous plant species. Similarly, tiny herps of a wide variety of species also will be at risk when housed in the company of such plants. Small invertebrates will be in danger as well because pitcher plants and other carnivorous plants are highly adapted to attracting and consuming invertebrate prey.

Of course, the threats posed by plants do not end with those carnivorous species. Many species of plants, especially tropical varieties, defend themselves from predation by secreting toxic or noxious saps and resins. Some of these resins deter herbivores merely by being sticky or distasteful, while others can be downright lethal. The thick white sap of the popular houseplant *Dieffenbachia* is extremely toxic, and if eaten, may cause symptoms ranging from swelling in the throat and jaws to coma and even death in some herbivorous species. Likewise, the berries and leaves of the robust terrarium plant English ivy may cause severe stress and uneasiness in herbivorous herps that consume them. Avoid mixing herbivorous herp species with plants that they may nibble upon at the risk of their own health. Losing a pet herp or invertebrate to a poisonous or otherwise dangerous plant isn't something that any hobbyist wants to go through.

Planting Methods

Once you've picked out the plant species you want, aligned their biological needs and compatibility within an ecosystem or plant community, and determined that they will neither be threatened nor pose a threat to your pet reptiles, amphibians, or invertebrates, it's time to think about anchoring or planting them within your terrarium.

In-Pot Planting

In-pot planting is a very simple method of anchoring that is recommended to beginning hobbyists who have low skill levels when raising live plants in the terrarium. In-pot planting involves digging a hole in the substrate of your terrarium that is large enough to accommodate a plant's entire pot, placing the plant, pot and all, in the hole, and entirely covering the pot with substrate. When finished, this method will give the *appearance* that your plant

Euphorbia produce a sticky sap when injured, so they must be used in terrariums with care.

is growing directly from the substrate of your naturalistic terrarium, but in reality, the plant is still safely anchored within the confines of its pot.

Many hobbyists replant their plants using fresh soil when conducting in-pot style plantings; I have done this, and unless the plant was originally anchored in very poor soil, I haven't noticed much of a difference between replanting and allowing the plant to remain in its original soil matrix inside the pot. Perhaps different species of plants might react differently, however. Removing the soil does help to eliminate the possibility of introducing ants or other undesirable organisms to the terrarium.

In-pot planting is especially advisable when anchoring a delicate, ailing, or special-needs plant in your terrarium. Any extra water or fertilizer that the plant should receive can simply be added directly to the potted soil so that that particular plant benefits without you having to change the entire chemical makeup of the terrarium's substrate. Very young plants or newly rooted cuttings also should be anchored by way of in-pot planting because they will definitely need to stay within the safety of their potting soil matrix while they mature, strengthen, and grow ample root systems to thrive outside of the pot.

Most plants anchored in a newly established naturalistic terrarium should be anchored in-pot. Newly established terrariums often lack the beneficial bacterial agents that help to maintain plant life. Until your tank matures to at least six to eight weeks old, it will have very little organic activity going on in the substrate; thus, your plants will likely suffer if planted directly into the biologically inactive substrate.

The dumb canes (*Dieffenbachia*) have toxic crystals in their sap, so they must not be used with any herps that might nibble them.

While in-pot planting is highly beneficial to young plants, seedlings, cuttings, and otherwise sensitive specimens, it does have definite drawbacks. Plants that are permanently anchored inside their pots will be greatly inhibited when it comes to growth rates. As the roots of your plants grow, they will become larger and longer. In the wild, these roots would spread out through the soil around them, but if left in the pot, the plant can easily become root-bound, the roots growing together in a tight and tangled knot. Root-bound plants have trouble absorbing nutrients and moisture.

Plants that are anchored in-pot also may be much slower to spread throughout the terrarium than those specimens that are anchored directly into the substrate. Most species of bamboo, for example, send underground runners out through the soil. These runners have nodes along their length, and from these nodes, new shoots of bamboo sprout from the soil. If your bamboo is kept within a pot, the runners will not be able to pass through the ground, and any new shoots will spring from within the pot, rather than spreading around your naturalistic terrarium. Many advanced hobbyists and vivarium purists also feel that adding plants that are still in their pots is an act that defies the "natural" aspect of the naturalistic terrarium.

It is usually easy to hide plant pots behind landscape features or beneath substrate.

A good solution to these problems is to anchor your plants in the terrarium using biodegradable pots, such as those made of thin cardboard or another loose, easily composted material. While the nonliving substrate is still inhospitable and biologically inactive, your plants will be protected, but as the substrate of your terrarium matures into a homogenous soil that is teeming with organic activity, the pots in which your plants are anchored will slowly rot away so that it will not be necessary to dig up and replant your vegetation. As the pot rots away, your plants will be free to spread their roots, expand their foliage, and flourish within your terrarium.

In-Substrate Planting

The next method, which advanced vivarium and naturalistic terrarium enthusiasts often prefer, is in-substrate planting. As its name suggests, in-substrate planting involves removing your plants from their pots and planting them directly in the substrate of the terrarium. For your plants to thrive when anchored directly into the substrate, the substrate itself must be

Pesticide Perils

While hobbyists often think about the agricultural and chemical pollutants that accompany the soils of newly purchased plants, they often overlook the leaves of those plants. A growing number of pesticides and fungicides are designed for use strictly on the leaves of most plants. Designed to kill herbivorous insects and some microbes, these chemicals can wreak utter havoc on the ecological balance of the terrarium once introduced into a tank. In fact, these leaf-borne chemicals are even more dangerous than their soil-borne counterparts due to the immediate proximity of the poisons to pets. Avoid this terrible scenario by washing the leaves of all living plants in cool, clean water before adding them into your naturalistic terrarium.

biologically active: beneficial bacteria, fungi, and mycorrhizae, which help the root hairs of your plant to absorb moisture and nutrients, must be present and alive in the substrate of your terrarium if your plants are to survive. For this reason, plants that are anchored in-substrate have a much better survival rate if they are added to a pre-existing terrarium, because many newly established tanks do not contain enough biological goodies to maintain plant life. A good way around this problem is to add large amounts of composting leaf matter to your terrarium mixture. Composting leaves are rich with beneficial microbials, and by adding a healthy portion of this material into your substrate mix you can speed up the maturation of your substrate.

There are far more benefits to in-substrate planting than there are drawbacks. In-substrate planting allows your plants to freely grow and flourish, much as they would in nature. Runners snake under the surface to sprout new chutes, roots fan out through the soil to gather nutrients and anchor the plant, tendrils and foliage branch out into the terrarium, and the cycle of life really gets revved up and running when your plants are anchored in-substrate.

As the roots of each plant expand, their collective biological impact can be felt throughout the entire tank. The wastes that your herp emits are rapidly processed and broken down into usable nitrogen products that are absorbed by the roots, so the pH of the soil is held in stasis. The more your plants flourish unbound within the substrate of your terrarium, the more self-sustaining and mature your terrarium will become. These qualities would not be achievable if all the plants in your terrarium were anchored in-pot.

The physical act of in-substrate planting is a pretty easy and straightforward task. Simply remove your chosen plant from its pot, and using the back of a spoon or other blunt object,

Some plants will spread throughout the terrarium when planted directly in the substrate. Devil's ivy has done so in this rainforest terrarium housing a temple viper.

gently tap the roots of your plant until most of the potting soil falls away.

Greenhouses and nurseries often use strong fertilizers to encourage plant growth. When planted in the outdoor flower garden or vegetable garden, these fertilizers have virtually no impact on the surrounding animal life, but when kept within the small confines of the terrarium, these same fertilizers can easily taint the water and soil, affecting any other life form that comes near them. Fertilizers, herbicides, pesticides, fungicides, and a host of other agricultural chemicals often accompany the potting soil. Once introduced into the ecosystem of your terrarium, these dangerous chemicals can wreak havoc on your plants, herps, invertebrates, and even the organic activity within your mature, living substrate. Never allow excess potting matrix into your terrarium.

But if potting soil poses such a threat to the ecology of your terrarium, why is it safe to conduct in-pot plantings in your tank? Won't that potting matrix contaminate the substrate? Not really. Because the pot itself acts like a buffer between the terrarium substrate and the potting soil, there is seldom any major chemical exchange between the two soils. Any harmful chemicals within the potting matrix slowly dissipate rather than suddenly bombarding the terrarium. Mature tanks are, however, more at risk than newly established terrariums when it comes to pollution by agricultural agents. Newly established terrariums aren't really living ecosystems yet, so there isn't a strong natural balance that can be destroyed. The mature, self-sustaining ecosystem that exists in an old and well-established terrarium, however, can be adversely affected by the trace amounts of chemicals exuding from the potting matrix of an in-pot planting. My best advice is to perform in-pot plantings only in young terrariums that do not have sufficient biological activity to support plant life, and to conduct in-substrate plantings in older, more mature systems or in young terrariums with viable, active substrate.

Eco-Planting

A third method of planting is something that I call eco-planting. Eco-planting involves some of the naturalistic décor within your terrarium acting as receptacles for the roots of your plants. A very simple form of eco-planting is applicable in the desert terrarium: Anchor a cow or steer skull on an angle in the substrate and fill the skull itself with sandy substrate until it is nearly exuding from the eye socket. Into this eye socket, plant a small species of cactus, such as strawberry cactus or a young sea-urchin cactus. This will give the effect of time and age in the terrarium, as well as an ironic symbol of life triumphing over death: the living cactus thriving in the skull of a dead animal. Bear in mind that bones and skulls must only be used in very arid terrarium because they tend to hold moisture and foster microbial growth when used in humid terrariums.

The Right Planting for the Right Plant

Not all species of plants lend themselves comfortably to all styles of planting. Some varieties fare very poorly if kept in a small pot, while others may not thrive if they are planted in open substrate without sufficient moisture surrounding their roots, as in in-substrate planting. Perhaps the narrowest of all fields is the eco-planting field. Unless all conditions are superior, only a few plant species will do well when eco-planted in a small nook or cranny within your terrarium. Make sure to study the planting needs of your chosen species of plants before you anchor them in your terrarium in an unsustainable manner. If you are in doubt about the needs of a specific plant, ask a horticultural expert or consult the Internet. Anchoring the right plant under the right conditions is critical to the long-term success of the plant life in your naturalistic terrarium.

Don't Let This Happen to You

A colleague of mine once established a thriving South American Jungle habitat that he modeled after the wilderness of Venezuela. He had imported plants indigenous to that area, maintained his substrate at the proper pH, and carefully selected his herps, a small community of *Dendrobates* frogs, also known as poison arrow or poison dart frogs. His colony of frogs thrived in their living vivarium for several years, living so much like they would in nature that they even spawned on numerous occasions.

In about the fourth year of the terrarium's life, my colleague added several plants directly into the terrarium's substrate without first removing the potting matrix in which the plants had been previously living. He planted them potting soil and all. Within a week's time he noticed that some of his frogs were acting sick: struggling to walk or hop upright, acting "drunk," and refusing food. It was not long before his beloved frogs began dying.

Around the same time, he also noticed that some of the plants within his tank were thriving. Leaves became fuller, stems put on new growth, and the algae growing in the pool at one end of the terrarium began growing at a highly accelerated rate. It was then that my colleague realized his mistake, and he knew what had killed his frogs. It was fertilizer. Synthetic fertilizer was mixed in the potting matrix, and when my colleague put that mixture into his substrate, the fertilizers soaked into the water column and fatally polluted his terrarium.

Another good example of eco-planting is the hollow log or slab of driftwood. A cured and properly conditioned piece of wood may have any number of naturally occurring holes, pits, and grooves. And if your chosen piece of wood doesn't naturally have such features, it is easy to chisel or carve holes into the wood. Special drill bits (known as hole saws) can drill large holes into a log or slab of driftwood in mere seconds. Once drilled, these holes can easily be enlarged by using a file or a rasp to widen or shape them to meet your desired specifications.

Once your piece of wood has sufficient holes in it, you may anchor it in the soil and plant a plant in the hole in a manner similar to that of the skull in the desert, or you may wish to try an alternate method of boring out the wood and filling the hollow with a deep layer of substrate. Once the substrate is thick enough to accommodate the root systems of

Devil's ivy (*Scindasus aureus*), also known as pothos, is a good candidate for eco-planting. Here, it has been planted in a cork bark hollow.

your chosen plant, you may anchor it into the log or slab of driftwood in such a manner that it appears that the plant is naturally growing directly from the log. In a true woodland or jungle environment, it is not at all uncommon to find small plants growing from the rotting pulp of an ancient log. In the home terrarium, however, it is very difficult to introduce large amounts of rotting wood without introducing the pathogens and bacteria that naturally occur within it. By hollowing out a nonrotting log and filling it with viable, healthy substrate, you can gain all the splendor and beauty of a log-sprouted plant without introducing all of the negative components into your tank.

One of my own favorite tactics is to hollow out a length of oak or hickory wood (both of which last much longer than pine or cedar, and they also lack the offensive resins and odors associated with evergreen woods) and fill the hollow with a mixture of 3 parts composting leaves, 1 part peat moss, 1 part shredded coconut husks, and 1 part nonsilica sand. This mixture is rich enough in nutrients to support a healthy stand of vegetation but also airy enough to encourage fast root development. Atop such a mixture I deposit a patchwork of moss clumps. I make sure to water the moss thoroughly and daily, because this virtually rootless plant will wither very quickly if deprived of ample moisture. As time passes, the borders of each moss clump will expand until they touch, and eventually they will entirely cover the surface of my hollowed-out log. This method of eco-planting only works if the log is laid flat across the substrate of the terrarium or if it is elevated at only a

The Eco-Wall

The naturalistic terrarium hobby is a growing segment of the herp hobby, and every time you turn around, it seems there's something new on the market. My favorite item that is gaining in popularity is the plantable wall, or eco-wall, as I like to call it. Made of compressed coconut husk, these porous, lightweight, moisture-retentive panels offer an excellent vertical habitat for bromeliads and arboreal orchids, which can be anchored directly into the walls. Similarly, climbing vines such as English ivy or variegated ivy do remarkably well when sending their tendrils slithering over the eco-wall. Some varieties of mosses grow well in such panels as well.

Manufactured by a number of companies, these panels come in a variety of sizes and can be cut to fit your tank. Simply cut the panels to the desired size and glue them to the inner walls of your terrarium using standard silicon aquarium sealant. By using some in your home terrarium, you can add a whole new dimension to the beauty and intrigue of your naturalistic jungle or tropical forest terrarium

very slight angle. Small ferns also may be rooted into a hollow log by way of this method.

Another style of eco-planting is very similar to this moss-planting tactic, but it involves vertically standing logs (which may come to resemble tree trunks). In the jungle habitat, a standing tree trunk or vertical log may be bored out in several places along its length. These holes should measure at least 1 inch (2.5 cm) deep by 1/2 inch (1.3 cm) wide. Small deposits of shredded coconut husk can be packed into these holes, and atop this mix, a small bromeliad can be inserted. Bromeliads, or "air plants" as they are sometimes known, occur naturally in the steamy jungles of Central and South America, and they need virtually no soil in which to grow. In the wild, bromeliads grow in the perpetually moist forks of trees high above the soil of the jungle floor, but in the captive terrarium, some continually moist shredded coconut husk will suffice because this type of substrate will supply the plants with ample moisture without choking them out or radically affecting the pH of their tiny roots as a heavier or thicker substrate would do. Secure these air plants by way of thread or fishing line; simply tie a small knot firmly, but not too tightly, around the base of the bromeliad, and tie the other end to an arboreal perch. A small patch of cleverly placed moss or bark will conceal the fishing line from view. Some hobbyists also use nontoxic glue to cement their bromeliads in place.

Small orchids also may be added to a standing bough in this manner. Instead of using shredded coconut husk, however, orchids should be anchored in sphagnum moss, which will keep the faint roots of the orchid damp. Simply mist the orchid and its surrounding moss with a handheld garden sprayer every second or third day. Known as "penthouse plants" because of their lofty station high above the floor of the terrarium, both bromeliads and orchids can add the perfect touch to an otherwise incomplete jungle terrarium. Make sure to plant them high in the tank to achieve an inspiring "jungle canopy" effect. Although they may not sound overly elaborate, these vertically situated plants can add a dramatic visual effect to the naturalistic terrarium.

Still another form of eco-planting is to anchor your plants within the nooks and crannies of a large rock or small boulder within the terrarium. Begin by anchoring a large stone deep in the terrarium substrate—deeply enough that it will not shift or fall. To accommodate a stand of living vegetation in or on its surface, this stone must have a pitted surface with one or more deep depressions or crevasses. Mexican lava rock is an excellent choice, as are certain formations of granite. Both Mexican lava and granite are fairly inert stones, and they will not easily decompose or radically raise the pH of your terrarium. Limestone, on the other hand, is a delicate stone comprised largely of calcium, and it will break down very quickly when exposed to water. Take great care when using limestone or a similar type of sedimentary rock. Eco-plant your chosen stone in the same manner that you

Err on the Side of Caution

When fertilizing your naturalistic terrarium, adding too little fertilizer is infinitely better than adding too much. Adding fertilizer to a terrarium is a lot like adding salt to a recipe: Once you've added too much, you can't unadd it, and you've likely ruined the recipe! Once the fertilizer is in your terrarium, especially if it was a liquid or fine powder, it's pretty well in there—you can't take it back out without tearing down your terrarium. Too much fertilizer can lead to the illness or death of your herps or invertebrates, and it can literally "burn up" your plant life; the high concentrations of the chemicals in the fertilizer are lethal to most vegetation. If you're unsure how much fertilizer to add, don't add anything or add only very small amounts—about one-quarter the amount recommended by the manufacturer.

Bromeliads—*Tilsandia caput-medusae* shown here—often do very well when eco-planted because they need little or no soil.

eco-planted your logs or hunks of driftwood: Fill the crevasse or depression in the rock with a substrate mixture that is appropriate for the type of plant you are anchoring in the rock. Sphagnum moss, peat moss, or coconut husks are a good choice for placing a bromeliad or two atop your rock, while a composting lea and sand mixture will accommodate a healthy stand of moss.

If the bowl or depression of the rock is deep enough, you may wish to anchor a species of plant that grows a larger root system, such as a *Peperomia* or a fern. I've seen some very attractive eco-plantings comprising a stone depression and a vine-type plant. Philodendron, for example, or some variety of ivy (variegated Canary Island ivy, for example) will grow a root system in the substrate of the rock's hollow and will send numerous tendrils crawling down the face of the stone and deeper into the terrarium. A fixture such as this can be a stunning, ancient-looking display; if the stone is situated at one of the highest points of the tank, its placement will accentuate the snake-like length of the plant's tendrils.

Bear in mind that all varieties of rock, even the most inert, will raise the pH of their surrounding substrate to some degree. And when that substrate is completely surrounded by rock, as it is in your eco-planted stone scenario, the plants you've anchored in the rock's depression may suffer over time. Most plant species can tolerate a relatively high pH, but if you anchor an acid-loving species in a rock bowl, use a substrate mixture with a low pH, such as peat moss or composting leaves. If your plants start to pale around their leaves or show signs of general wilting, they are succumbing to the high-mineral, high-pH content of the stone bowl. Remove the plants, replace their substrate with a fresh batch of a low pH mixture, and water the plant thoroughly to rinse away the offending chemicals.

Terrarium backgrounds made of coconut husk and cork bark are available, enabling hobbyists to anchor plants to the back wall of the terrarium, as shown here with a *Dendrobates tinctorius*.

Final Thoughts on Planting

Each of these anchoring methods—in-pot, in-substrate, and eco-planting—has its pros and its cons, and ultimately it is up to you to decide which avenue is best for your terrarium. Many vivarium purists and serious hobbyists prefer to use solely one method over the other, although I feel that a hybrid method—a mixture that incorporates the strengths and benefits of each—of naturalistic terrarium construction is also a great choice. Some of your more delicate or high-maintenance plants can be planted in-pot so that you can give them the additional care and nutrients that they may require while still maintaining the environmental status quo within the remainder of your terrarium. Strong, healthy, robust plants, as well as those varieties that are very hardy and easy to cultivate (such as *Philodendron* or *Dieffenbachia*) may be planted in-substrate and allowed to roam, grow, flourish, and wander through the terrarium as they will. And eco-planting can achieve aesthetic effects unattainable by either of the other two methods of anchoring. A truly well-rounded vivarium or naturalistic terrarium will incorporate all three methods of planting.

Plant Maintenance

Once your plants are anchored in your terrarium, you now face the never-ending duty of maintenance. Don't let the phrase "never-ending duty" fool you, however, because the cultivation of terrarium plants can be exciting and enjoyable; watching the plants grow, pruning them back, and even crafting them and shaping them into the forms you desire for

Tilsandia and many other bromeliads can be attached to a piece of bark or other terrarium decoration with some fishing line or a bit of glue.

your terrarium can be relaxing and rewarding tasks. One of the foremost concerns when dealing with plants in the terrarium is watering. That topic, however, is covered in the "Water & Watering" chapter.

Fertilizing

For our purposes in this chapter, the first matter of plant maintenance is fertilizing and fertilizers. What types of fertilizers are safe for use in the naturalistic terrarium? How do you properly measure and apply fertilizers? How often should fertilizer be added, and what types of plants need more or less fertilizers? These can be daunting questions that, if not properly addressed, can have harmful or even fatal ramifications to your plants and herps or invertebrates. And of course, not all types of vivarium or naturalistic terrarium will even require that additional fertilizers be added.

The best advice that I can give is to begin your selection of fertilizers by fully understanding the animals that live in your terrarium. Some species of herps or invertebrates are more sensitive to fertilizers and other chemicals, while other species are far more resilient to even harsh fertilizers. The proximity and degree of contact that occur between your herps and your fertilizers also will have a serious impact on things. As a general rule, amphibians are much more likely to be sensitive to fertilizers, so the use of fertilizers in an amphibian enclosure is risky.

Another potential problem that can arise with fertilizers is the matter of ingestion. Most reptiles and amphibians will not intentionally ingest chemical fertilizers, but accidental ingestion occurs more often than you might think. Obvious conditions that make an animal more prone to accidental ingestion concern the animal's diet and eating habits. If your pet herp is an herbivore, like a green iguana or a tortoise, you must take care when using foliar fertilizers because the presence of the leaves and the herp's tendencies to munch on leaves

Hold the Salt!

Many synthetic fertilizers contain mineral salts, which can be detrimental to life within your terrarium. Mineral salts are added to synthetic fertilizers as a catalyst that helps plants absorb the rest of the fertilizer's elements in a swift manner. Fertilizers with these salts usually are labeled "fast acting." When used in the home terrarium, salt-containing fertilizers are extremely dangerous, causing dehydration and chemical imbalances in the animals and eventually withering the plants. When selecting a fertilizer, watch out for the words "chloride," "sodium," "salt," and words ending in the suffix "-ate," such as phosphate or sulfate. All these words are red flags that indicate the presence of mineral salts in the fertilizer.

can be a dangerous combination. The herps also can ingest fertilizer by drinking water droplets that have absorbed the chemicals.

A second issue to consider when dealing with fertilizers is the needs of your plants. Not all species of plants need or require (or can even tolerate) the same types of fertilizer. This is another instance when the concept of the "plant community" comes into play. Housing multiple plant types that have highly varied requirements when it comes to fertilizers can be a chemistry nightmare when it comes time to fertilize. Some plants need more nitrogen, other need more phosphorous, and still others are virtually intolerant of heavy doses of nitrogen. If you've mixed a hodgepodge of plants in your terrarium with dissimilar fertilizer needs, chances are slim that all plants will thrive when exposed to the same fertilizer types and dosages. When you organize your terrarium with plants of similar nutrient needs, however, fertilizing can be a very easy task because all plants within a tank can be satisfied with a single dosage.

Some fertilizers are better and safer to use in the naturalistic terrarium than are others. And some are downright poisonous; these harsh toxins must be avoided at all costs. Knowing the difference between the types of fertilizers and knowing when and how to apply them is key to giving your plants the extra nutrients they may need, while at the same time ensuring the health and survival of your herps or invertebrates.

Synthetic Fertilizer Sometimes referred to as "media" fertilizer, synthetic fertilizer is sold at department stores, hardware stores, and nurseries across the country. These granulated fertilizers are not always suitable for use within the mature naturalistic terrarium, although small amounts can be successfully employed during the initial setup of the terrarium to give your plants a little "spurt" of extra nutrients while they are establishing their root systems within the terrarium substrate. Tanks housing aquatic frogs and salamanders should not be fertilized with synthetic fertilizers while the inhabitants of the tank are present.

These fertilizers are typically harsh and are designed for use in large, open areas such as gardens and lawns. They can easily be overused in the enclosed terrarium, the end result being burned plants and heavy buildup of nitrogen and other elements, which can lead to respiratory and dermal injury in some herps. Amphibians are particularly sensitive to synthetic fertilizers. Novice hobbyists should avoid these harsh chemicals and use safer, slower-acting varieties.

Organic Fertilizer A more gentle form of fertilizer to add to a thriving terrarium is the organic fertilizer. Made from the shells and remains of plants and animals, these chemicals contain naturally benign elements that are typically safe for most of the reptile and amphibian inhabitants in your terrarium. Organic fertilizers are very long lasting; thus, it will take your plants a longer time to absorb and process all their nutrients. The plants themselves will not be able to directly absorb the nutrients from these fertilizers in their current form; these nutrients must first be broken down and transformed into a more basic form by the fungi and bacteria living in the substrate before the plants will be able to absorb them. This process is natural and very safe for

Time to Fertilize?

Not all naturalistic terrariums require the addition of extra fertilizers. Terrariums that have an ample supply of animal life in them may not need fertilizers because the wastes of your herps will be processed and utilized by the root systems of your plants, thereby providing your plants with ample nitrogen, phosphorous, and other nutrients. If your plants are green, healthy, and seem to be putting on new leaves and longer stems, no fertilizer is necessary.

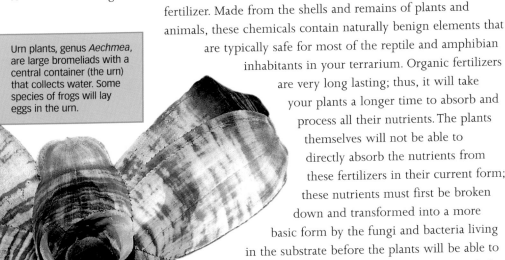

Urn plants, genus *Aechmea*, are large bromeliads with a central container (the urn) that collects water. Some species of frogs will lay eggs in the urn.

Fertilize your terrarium with utmost caution. Fertilizers may be toxic to your animals, especially amphibians like this Madagascar reed frog.

the animals living in your tank; the decomposition and absorption of the fertilizer's nutrients will occur in your terrarium almost exactly as it would in the wild. For this reason, organic fertilizers are very forgiving in their dosages. Because this type of fertilizer requires a strong presence of microbes in the terrarium, you will not see any immediate effects if you add organic fertilizer to a newly established tank in which biological activity is fairly low.

Foliar Fertilizer Foliar fertilizer is usually sold as a liquid, but it is occasionally encountered in a finely powdered form. Formulated to be easily absorbed through the pores and thin membranous tissue of most leaves, foliar fertilizers are very fast acting supplementary fertilizers, aiding leaves and foliage in obtaining nutrients that they might not be getting from animal wastes or other root-absorbable fertilizers. If used properly, foliar fertilizers are especially beneficial to rootless plants such as mosses, bromeliads, and some types of orchids.

Designed to be mixed with water in a large spray bottle, foliar fertilizers must be used with caution, especially in the presence of amphibians and lizards that lap water droplets from leaves. The best time to apply this style of fertilizer is in the early morning, soon after you turn on the terrarium's lights. During this time, the leaves of each plant in the terrarium are "waking up" for the day. With their cells working and photosynthesis in full swing, each leaf is ready to absorb some fertilizer. If you have amphibians or small lizards, make sure that they cannot come into direct contact with the freshly sprayed leaves—remove the herps to a secondary terrarium if necessary. Once the foliar fertilizer is dry, you

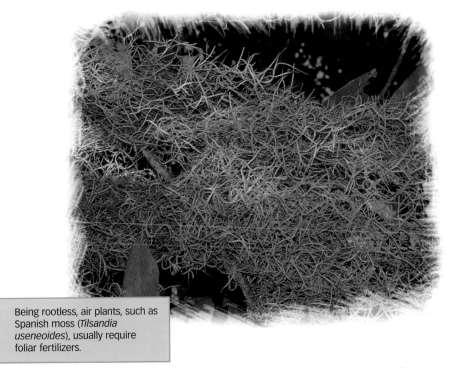

Being rootless, air plants, such as Spanish moss (*Tilsandia useneoides*), usually require foliar fertilizers.

may place the herps in their freshly fertilized home. To ensure that your herps are not subsequently injured through contact with the fertilized leaves, mix the foliar fertilizer at one-quarter or one-fifth the strength that is recommended on the package. Such a diluted mixture is much safer for use around your animals.

Aquatic Fertilizer In swamp and bog terrariums, still another type of fertilizer can come in handy. Designed specifically for use in koi ponds and heavily planted aquariums, aquatic fertilizer is easily the safest formula that you could ever use in your naturalistic terrarium. Appearing for sale in pet shops and specialty nurseries as liquids or dissolving tabs, these fertilizers will do wonders for the mature naturalistic terrarium because they are not harsh but are relatively fast acting. Of course, tadpoles, frogs, toads, salamanders, and other amphibians are quite sensitive to chemical reagents, so use only one-third or one-quarter the concentration recommended on the package inside the home terrarium. Aquatic fertilizer is excellent at providing added nutrients for duckweed, water hyacinth, water lettuce, lilies, and arrow plants.

Chapter 6

Water and Watering

The element of water and the act of watering the terrarium are some of the most advanced aspects of properly maintaining the naturalistic terrarium. It seems so simple, yet so many hobbyists find themselves frustrated and frazzled when their attempts to add water to their terrarium go frightfully awry—substrate flooding, plants dying, herps stressing, and the terrarium smelling foul. As is true of all other aspects of the naturalistic terrarium, however, "getting it right" when it comes to water and watering is simply a matter of understanding water and knowing how it will behave in your home terrarium.

Amphibians are especially sensitive to water quality. A Chinese dwarf newt (*Cynops orientalis*) is shown here with a sword plant.

Types of Water

Let's begin by discussing the types of water available. There are five major types of water that most hobbyists might consider using in the home terrarium: distilled, city, well, rain, and bottled springwaters. Each of these types has its pros and cons, and each is more or less applicable to the type of terrarium you have established. Once you begin watering the plants in your terrarium with a particular type of water, you should continue using only that type. Switching suddenly to a different type of water that has a radically different chemical or mineral content can send your plants into shock and may kill off the beneficial bacteria and fungi living in your substrate mix.

Distilled Water

Distilled water is manufactured by rapidly evaporating a tank of water in a lab, then recollecting the water vapor from the atmosphere in a separate container. As the water evaporates, all the minerals and nutrients that it contained are left behind, and only the pure water is collected and bottled. This water has no minerals, no nutrients, and virtually nothing else that your plants need to grow and thrive. Distilled water also can harm any aquatic amphibians you may be keeping

Distilled water can be useful when you are keeping plants, such as carnivorous types, that have strict pH requirements. The neutral pH of distilled water keeps it from affecting the soil's pH. In most other cases, though, avoid distilled water.

City Water

City water is any type of water that is pumped through municipal pipes and processed at purification, sewage treatment, or desalinization plants, or that is chemically treated in any way. City water is, for the most part, some of the worst water you could possibly add to your living terrarium, because it almost certainly contains dangerous chemicals, including chlorine and fluoride. Chlorinated city water may prove fatal to fully aquatic amphibians, such as tadpoles and newts.

If you absolutely must water your terrarium with city water, make it less dangerous by letting it sit out in an open container for 24 hours. During this time, most of the chlorine and fluoride ions will escape into the atmosphere, and the water will be purer. You can also add aquarium dechlorinator to the water, which will remove chlorine and ammonia but not fluoride.

City Water Blues

Because city water contains so much chlorine and fluoride, it is harmful to both the plant life in your terrarium, as well as some forms of herps. Amphibians that spend a good deal of time swimming in or submerged under water, such as tadpoles, newts, and larval salamanders, are particularly at risk. If chlorine- and fluoride-rich waters are added to tanks containing these animals, the result is likely going to be a sick or even slain herp. Treat any city waters with an aquarium-suitable dechlorinator before adding them to the pools and ponds of your terrarium.

Well Water

Drawn from deep within the earth's bedrock layers, well water is typically very high in minerals and dissolved elements, particularly calcium, sodium, and sulfur (It is often called "hard water.") Well water works well in most desert-style terrariums, the soil of which is already very high in mineral content.

The high mineral content (which equates to a high pH) within well water makes it unsuitable for many jungle or bog terrariums that need to maintain controlled levels of mineral content and stable (low) pH levels. When sprayed upon the leaves of some ferns and broad-leafed varieties of plants, well water may leave behind unsightly mineral residue on the leaves. Well water also may be high in dangerous metals such as copper or zinc. My advice is to get an aquarium water-quality test kit and test a sample for metal content before you add any well water to your terrarium. If high levels of copper or other metals are present, don't use this water.

Rainwater

Rainwater can be the best type of water you could ever add to your naturalistic terrarium. The process of rain formation cleanses the water of most naturally occurring impurities. Collect it with a tarp that drains into a plastic or glass bucket or other large container. Do not use a metal container for collecting rainwater, because trace amounts of the metal will leach into the water and can cause problems inside your terrarium. Before adding any of this collected rainwater into your terrarium, make sure to pour it through a coffee filter or other very fine seine to remove any bits of debris or drowned insects that may be present. One of the most advantageous aspects of using rainwater is the amount of additional nitrogen it contains, which will stimulate plant growth.

If you live in an area that suffers from acid rain, you should probably avoid using rainwater. Make sure that any rainwater you collect and use in your terrarium has a pH of no less than 6.2 to 6.8. Any pH reading lower than this is bordering on dangerously acidic. Alkaline pH can be just as dangerous to the delicate root systems of your plants and soft skins of your captive animals. A pH above 7 is too high. If you collect rainwater for use in your terrarium, purchase a pH test kit from your local pet shop and test all water samples before adding them to your tank.

Springwater

Available at virtually every retail grocery store on the planet, bottled springwater is a fine source of water to use in the terrarium. Do not confuse this with bottled purified water, which is nearly the same as distilled water. When buying springwater, pay close attention to the label. Suitable springwater will contain no added minerals, sodium, or other chemical preservatives, flavors, or other additives.

Some arboreal reptiles may only drink water when misted. Chameleons, such as this panther chameleon, are notorious for this behavior.

Watering Plants and Animals

Now that you know a little more about the different water types that are available, there are a few methods that you can use to keep your tank alive and healthy. Primarily, there are two major ways to water your plants: misting with a spray bottle or pouring water directly at the base of each plant.

Mist That Moss

Moss is an excellent plant to introduce into the home terrarium, and many hobbyists do so with high levels of success. However, moss is a primitive type of plant that lacks the root systems present in higher plants, and it is also completely devoid of a vascular system, which, in complex plants, transports nutrients and water from the soil out to the plant's leaves and stems. Mosses obtain their water from direct contact with moisture. As beads of water droplets sit atop the green tufts of foliage, tiny ducts or pores within the moss open to absorb the water.

For this reason, you must mist any mosses in your terrarium daily. The hobbyist who simply pours water around the base of his mosses will soon notice the moss darkening, drying, and withering. The good news is that most moss species are highly drought tolerant, so a seemingly dead clump of moss can usually be revived through a series of mistings sprayed directly onto its foliage.

Misting

Misting consists of spraying down either all or part of the inside of the terrarium with clean, ambient-temperature water. It's that simple. Just spray down the leaves of your plants until the droplets on each leaf are big enough to fall to the substrate below. Depending on what types of plants and animals you house in your terrarium, daily mistings may be more or less important, and may need to occur more or less frequently. The desert terrarium might benefit from a very mild early morning misting once a week or less often. A tropical forest terrarium will require moderate misting to be performed once daily. And the terrarium that houses arboreal geckos, anoles, or chameleons will require more frequent mistings performed at regular intervals throughout the day, because these lizards drink water not from a standing dish but by lapping up tiny droplets.

Pouring

The second type of watering is simply to pour a small amount of water at the base of each plant. This method is highly variable depending on which type of naturalistic terrarium you maintain. Desert foliage, depending on the exact species, needs to be watered only once or twice every few weeks, so a small amount of water administered directly at the base of each plant will help to sustain it without adding excess moisture into the substrate of the tank. Conversely, jungle and swamp terrariums will be planted with species that demand almost continual moisture, so rather than pouring a little water at the base of each plant, you should maintain a sufficiently moist substrate at all times.

Avoid overwatering by not watering all the plants in a terrarium at the same time. If your plants are planted directly in the substrate, by watering each plant on the same day, your substrate will become sopping wet. For most terrarium types, this is not a good thing.

Plants in the naturalistic terrarium are not growing in isolation, so the watering needs of all can be satisfied with a smaller amount water. The water given to one plant will soak into the soil and reach the root systems of the others. A good way to think about watering is that each plant in your terrarium is rooted in the same "pot" as all the other plants. In-pot and eco-planted plants are exceptions, of course.

A good way to avoid overwatering is to stagger the times and dates that you water your terrarium plants. Perhaps you could water two out of four plants in your terrarium and then water the other two the next time. Each terrarium is different, and it will take some trial and error to get the watering schedule right. By closely observing the plants and how they respond, you will be able to arrive at the proper watering schedule. It is usually better to err on the side of the terrarium being too dry, especially in a desert terrarium.

It is almost always better to err on the side of keeping your terrarium plants too dry, especially when dealing with aloes and other desert species.

Another excellent method for regulating the amount of water in your terrarium is to apply some type of ground cover—any thick, natural material that will help your substrate retain moisture—over the floor of the tank. In the woodland terrarium, a layer of only slightly composted leaves can be spread about 1 inch (2.5 cm) thick over the substrate. The uppermost leaves will remain dry, while the lower leaves will be moister, and the substrate mix beneath them will be kept adequately moist.

Another good rule of thumb when watering your terrarium is to portion out only small amounts of liquid each time you water. For example, if you notice that your Japanese *Fatsia* is looking a little droopy for lack of water, pour only a small amount around its base and wait six to eight hours. If the plant still droops, add a little more water until the *Fatsia* perks back up again. Try to avoid drenching the plants in your tank when you think they need some water. You can always add more water until your plants perk up again, but you can't easily remove any water from the substrate once you've added too much.

Evaporative Water Table

A third style of watering is only suitable for certain types of terrariums. I call it the "evaporative water table," and it refers to the amount of liquid water or

Amphibians that require very high relative humidity, such as mantellas, will benefit from an evaporative water table in the terrarium.

water vapor that is in the tank at any given time. It is more or less a constant, and advanced hobbyists find that this method of watering takes a great deal of work and hassle out of the maintenance of the tank. Of course, not all terrariums can sustain a permanent water table. Deserts, savannas, woodlands, and some montane environments will not survive if subjected to watering by way of a permanent water table.

This is best suited to amphibian life over reptilian or invertebrate life due to the continual moisture accumulating on the surfaces of all items within the terrarium. Most reptiles and invertebrates cannot thrive long term in so moist an environment. Establish an evaporative water table simply by covering about two-thirds of the terrarium lid with a solid, impermeable substance, such as glass or plastic. Then add a healthy amount of water to the substrate and cover the tank. As the water in the terrarium slowly evaporates out of the substrate, the impermeable glass or acrylic covering over most of the terrarium lid will prevent it from merely escaping into the atmosphere as it normally would. Instead, the lid will trap the gaseous water vapor and cause it to condense into liquid droplets on the walls of the terrarium and on the leaves of the plants. When these droplets become heavy enough, they will rain back down into the substrate of the terrarium and again soak down to the root systems of your plants.

This concept of the perpetually moist vivarium is suitable to most jungle habitats sporting frog and salamander inhabitants. Its benefits include the limited worries of watering the tank. The hobbyist seldom has to add any additional water to the terrarium or worry about the humidity level in the tank fluctuating rapidly. Despite these benefits, the evaporative water table has its drawbacks as well.

Because the water vapor will be constantly accumulating on the glass walls of the terrarium, the hobbyist's ability to see into the tank will be somewhat compromised. Another drawback is the accumulation of wastes within the terrarium. As your captive amphibians excrete urine and feces into the tank, these nitrogenous wastes will break down and become part of the evaporative water table. The result will be a smelly, polluted rain that falls back down into the tank. The more animal life you have in your terrarium (or the smaller the terrarium), the worse this problem will become. In a large tank that has only a few, small amphibians, the problem may not occur at all

Curb the pollution of the evaporative water column by removing the impermeable lid from the terrarium for 8 to 12 hours once each week and by wiping away all condensation from the inside of the tank's glass walls. This will allow any noxious ammonia or nitrogenous gases to dissipate into the atmosphere, while at the same time allowing a wave of fresh

Including a pool or pond in your terrarium allows you the option of housing some aquatic and semi-aquatic species, such as bullfrogs.

Escape Routes

If you construct some type of permanent pool or pond in your terrarium, create several "escape routes" for your herps to utilize should they wander into the pool. Many species of reptiles are less than graceful when it comes to swimming and navigating in a pool of water; chameleons, small skinks, land-going turtles and tortoises, and virtually all species of hatchling herps are particularly at risk of drowning in an inescapable pool of water. Even excellent swimmers, such as tree frogs, baby monitor lizards, and adult salamanders can quickly tire and drown in a pond that has no means of exit.

Of course, the same vertical limb or vine that would allow a green tree frog to escape from a pond would do very little to help a struggling eastern box turtle get out of the pond. For this reason, the style of escape route that you use must work for your particular species of herp. Large, heavy-bodied herps, such as turtles and large lizards, will do well with merely a ramp or gently sloping shoreline as a means of escape, while a snake or tree frog can suffice with a few sturdy, rough-textured branches or vines extending into the pool. In the case of aquatic frogs, a few floating plants, such as water hyacinth or water lettuce, can serve as adequate escape routes.

air to sweep through the terrarium. Mist down the surface of the leaves and the substrate with fresh, clean water immediately prior to replacing the impermeable lid atop the terrarium.

Obviously, this method of watering is only applicable in terrariums in which both the plant life and the animal life will tolerate perpetually damp conditions. Even though these amphibians do thrive in moist conditions, a solid quarter of the terrarium lid must be left uncovered to allow for ample ventilation. The branches, plants, and hides located directly beneath this ventilated area will remain much drier than the rest of the tank and will offer dry refuge for any water-weary amphibians seeking a spot in which they can escape the excess moisture.

Ponds and Pools

Like most aspects of terrarium construction, water may be manipulated in a wide variety of ways to accommodate the desires of more advanced terrarium enthusiasts. Ponds and

A Word on Filters

Filtering all pools of standing water in your terrarium is very important. Mature systems in which there is plenty of biofiltration occurring (through the roots of live plants and other organic systems) may need less secondary mechanical and chemical filtration, but newly established systems will need all the filtration they can get to prevent the water from becoming foul.

Of course, not every filter is appropriate for every terrarium habitat. Fully submersible power filters, which draw in water at an extreme rate, flush it through media of activated carbon or nitro-chips, and then forcibly expel it out an exhaust vent back into the water column. They are well suited for large tanks containing large turtles, adult aquatic snakes, small crocodilians, and other large herps that are not in danger of being sucked into or otherwise harmed by the motorized filter. When housing tadpoles, aquatic salamanders, or other small or fragile species, a motorized submersible filter is not an option. Although not remotely as efficient as their motorized counterpart, air-driven foam filters are excellent choices for fragile animals. Fully submersible, these filters use a trickle of air bubbles to displace water inside the tank and gradually draw water through a dense sponge. All particulates in the water column are trapped in the pore network of the sponge, while clean water is expelled.

pools of standing or circulating water are good examples of such advanced techniques. By mastering the construction of these aquatic works of art, a hobbyist opens the door to many previously unavailable reptile and amphibian species. For example, semi-aquatic species such as mature tiger salamanders, sirens, newts, and a wide range of aquatic snakes may now be housed with a much higher degree of naturalistic comfort for the animal and in a much more aesthetically attractive habitat. Bear in mind, though, that building an advanced water structure, such as a pond or shoreline, is best drafted into the original plans of the tank; it is much more difficult to add a naturalistic pool into a pre-existing tank than it is to construct a pool into a terrarium during its initial formation.

Pond Construction

Construct a pond within your terrarium by excavating almost all substrate out of one portion of it. Most hobbyists prefer to excavate one end of the tank, because this makes the

You can divide your terrarium into land and water sections by attaching a piece of glass or plexiglass to the sides of the terrarium with silicone aquarium sealant, as seen in this terrarium.

construction of the pond somewhat easier. Advanced hobbyists may establish thriving pools at both ends of the tank, leaving a raised portion of land in the middle as a sort of vivarium island. Still other hobbyists may take the opposite route to pond construction and may excavate a small hole in the center of the tank that is completely surrounded by substrate mix. This method allows for only minimal viewing of the pond and its inhabitants; because the pond abuts no glass wall of the terrarium, the hobbyist can only view the pond by looking down on it from above, not in through the glass.

You also can establish a long, narrow pool that runs the entire length of the terrarium along the front wall. By pushing all the substrate toward the back of the tank, the excavated area will be a strip along the front wall. This method is one of my personal favorites, because it creates a very unique appearance and allows for maximum visibility of the pool and its underwater inhabitants.

Whatever style of pool or pond you decide to build, it's important to follow a few guidelines to make it a living, thriving body of water and not merely a stagnant, putrid puddle in your tank.

Begin by excavating a desired portion of substrate from the terrarium. Remove most organic substrate mix (like coconut husks and bark chips), because these items will not remain stationary in the presence of liquid water; they will continually float and clutter the pool. Pile your substrate fairly high throughout the rest of the terrarium—you'll want plenty of dry land for your herps to live on after you've constructed the pond. I recommend leaving a layer of pea gravel or sand in the bottom of the excavated area, which will become the flooring of the pool.

A Shoreline Construction Method

One friend of mine created a beautiful woodland tank with a unique shoreline. In this woodland tank, she figured out an ingenious way to permanently separate the tank's water from the tank's dry land.

She began by building a small wooden ramp that fit (in width) perfectly and snugly in her tank. She then placed smooth, flat river rocks onto the ramp and glued them together with a nontoxic bonding sealant. She glued the rocks only to one another and not to the wooden ramp. She added more and more stones like pieces of a puzzle until the ramp was completely covered. She allowed the structure to dry, then lifted it carefully out of the tank. She then removed the ramp and added her substrate mixture to half of the tank, making sure to slope the substrate toward what would become the water end of the tank. When all was ready, she carefully placed the rocky "shoreline" structure atop the sloping substrate mix and then added the water until the rocky shoreline structure was more than halfway submerged.

The end result was an amazing terrarium in which the substrate stayed moist (the shoreline did not seal the land completely, but it formed a tight enough seal to prevent bits of substrate from flowing back into the pool), and the water stayed clean and clear. Her permanent shoreline structure worked perfectly. After a while, algae started growing on the artificially constructed shoreline, and the entire structure could not have looked more natural. Aquatic salamanders rested in the shallows of the shoreline, while tadpoles munched and nibbled at the algae that grew upon its cemented stones—further proof that when it comes to constructing naturalistic stone structures for the home terrarium, the sky's the limit!

The next step is to establish a stable shoreline. The easiest and quickest way to do this is to place several large, flat, smooth stones against the sloping wall of substrate. These rocks will anchor the substrate mix in place and prevent it from eroding and collapsing into the pool once it is filled with water. Construct this shoreline with an ample amount of stones, because it will not be complete until virtually no amount of substrate mix is visible along the shoreline. Plenty of water will seep through these rocks to soak the soil, but you don't want any substrate to flow back into the pool and pollute or cloud it.

Once these rocks are firmly in place, gently and slowly pour room-temperature water into the pool until the water level is approximately 2 to 3 inches (5 to 7.6 cm) *below* the top of the substrate. It may take a while to pour in enough water—and only enough water—to reach this point, because your substrate mixture may repel or soak it up, depending on its composition. At any rate, pour the water in slowly so that you don't pour in too much. Once the water is about 2 to 3 inches (5 to 7.6 cm) below the top of the substrate, stop adding it. This layer of dry substrate will act as the dry land that your herps will live on and in which the plants of your terrarium will remain firmly anchored. Beneficial bacteria and fungi also will have a space in which they can thrive. As you maintain your terrarium, make sure that the water level does not rise above this line, or you'll risk throwing off the ecological balance within the dry zone of your terrarium's substrate.

Pond Filtration

Of course, this pool and its water will not stay clean and viable for long without some type of filtration system. Older, more established terrariums that are cross-hatched with the thriving root systems of many plants may be able to filter the pond simply by virtue of the amount of roots that are tapped into the water column, but most hobbyists are well advised to add some form of mechanical filtration to the pond.

If you keep aquatic turtles in your terrarium, a filter will be essential. This is a hatchling chicken turtle.

In a brightly lit terrarium pool, duckweed will grow and spread over the water. It is shown here with a southern leopard frog.

Depending on the size of your terrarium and its inhabitants, you have a wide variety of mechanical filters from which to choose. If you have a shallow tank with aquatic turtles living in it, a hang-on style filter will do nicely. Simply attach the filter to the back or side of the tank, extend its intake stem into the depths of the pool, and turn it on. Make sure that this filter is fitted with appropriate activated carbon filtering media to remove ammonia and other nitrogenous wastes from the water column.

If, however, your terrarium houses a small aquatic snake or other herp that could escape through the gap created by the hang-on filter, then a fully submersible filter will be a much more viable option. This style of filter is a small, rectangular box that functions only when totally submerged under water. Again, make sure that it is outfitted with ample filtration media, sink it into the pool, and plug its cord into the nearest socket. This style of filter leaves only its thin cord running out through the lid (which can usually be cut to accommodate the cord), so the chances of your herps escaping from their home are minimal.

A final type of filter you might want to consider is the air-foam filter. Driven solely by air currents and water displacement, these filters have no moving parts and present no threat to small or delicate herps, such as axolotls, newts, salamander larvae, and tadpoles. These animals can easily be injured or even killed by the powerful intake currents generated by both the hang-on style and submersible-style filters, yet they are in absolutely no danger when housed in the company of a benign air-foam filter. Many hobbyists who breed some type of amphibian or another absolutely swear by the air-foam filter; its current is very weak, it has no mechanical gears, and it poses no danger to aquatic herps. Of course, the downside to this type of filter is its poor level of efficiency in cleaning the water of the pool. These filters simply cannot cope with large loads of waste.

Whichever style of filtration you choose, a filter must be present in your pool during the first few months after its construction. As time passes, the plant roots will grow down into the substrate, and when they grow beyond the line of the liquid water table, they will begin to biologically filter the water column, just like wild plants do in nature.

You will have to be very careful in the plant species you choose for such a purpose, because many species cannot tolerate a permanent water table around their roots. Some excellent varieties include bamboo, arrowhead, devil's ivy, pennywort, sedge, and sweet flag. Duckweed, water clover, water lettuce, frogbit, azolla, and water hyacinth all do wonders for both aesthetics and for cutting back on maintenance within the terrarium pond. Fully aquatic plants, such as eel grass, also may be incorporated into the pond.

Self-Contained Ponds

If you've read to this point, fallen in love with the idea of establishing a pool or pond in your naturalistic terrarium, and are now cursing yourself for having established an arid savanna terrarium that will not support a pond such as those described thus far, there's no need for worry. You can still build a pond in your tank. Many hobbyists establish elaborate and gorgeous ponds and pools within their savanna or woodland terrarium every year, and they meet with great success in doing so. The only difference between what they establish and the pond-building methods I've described thus far is that, while the water in my pond flows through the entire tank in a liquid water table, their ponds are perfectly contained in a bowl or dish that is anchored up

Some terrestrial plants will grow hydroponically in the pool of a terrarium, as devil's ivy is doing in this terrarium that houses a tiger salamander and some tree frogs.

to its rim in the terrarium. No pond water ever comes into direct contact with the substrate surrounding the pond. Because savanna terrariums must maintain a fairly low humidity, ponds should only be included in large setups. If in doubt, use a humidity gauge to make sure that your pond doesn't make the humidity in the tank too high.

To construct a contained pond, begin by finding a suitable bowl, dish, or other item that will act as the basin. Choose something that is sturdy and that is constructed out of a thick, long-lasting material. Avoid thin plastic, which can easily crack under weight or excessive stress. Thick plastic, acrylic, or even a glass container will suffice. Black or dark green items work well, because they blend in well with the aesthetics of most woodland terrariums, while a clear dish works best in a desert or savanna tank; the substrate visible through the glass bowl will naturally camouflage the glass, making it appear as if the pond is actually in the tank and not in a dish. I've found that clear cooking ware, such as Pyrex, works well for this purpose, as does Mexican bowl lava.

Once you've found a suitable item to act as the bowl of the pond, you'll need to determine where in the tank you want it. I recommend placing it centrally in the tank, a good distance away from any of the glass walls of the tank. You won't be able to see into the sides of the pond for an underwater view as you would in an in-terrarium pond, so placing the bowl close to the wall of the tank is unnecessary and unsightly.

Once you've planned where the bowl will sit, excavate that area of the terrarium substrate and seat the dish low enough in the tank so that the substrate comes to about 1/8 inch (0.3 cm) above the lip of the dish. This method of countersinking the lip of the dish will be useful later when you fully assimilate the dish into the topography of the terrarium.

Once the dish is seated into the substrate, you can begin camouflaging it and making it appear not as an obtrusive dish but as a perfectly natural pool of water within the terrarium. Fill the dish with water, and place within it a small, fully submersible aquarium filter or an air-foam filter (outfitted with adequate filtration media), depending on the needs of your herps.

Next, conceal the lip of the pond and break up its outline. If you're adding this dish to a woodland tank, placing several clumps of moss and a few flat stones around the border of the dish will conceal it from view and give the appearance that the pond is a quiet woodland pool that's always been there. As time passes, the moss will spread and more thoroughly cover the edge of the dish, giving it an "ancient" appearance. Dropping several fronds of duckweed into the pool will also enhance its biological activity and natural appearance. If you're establishing this pool in a savanna terrarium, ring the edge of the dish in flat stones, or plant a few small succulents in the substrate around the edge of the dish, giving the appearance of an oasis. In either case, hide the cord of the submersible filter by burying it in a shallow trench just beneath the surface of the substrate or ground cover.

Pond Maintenance

When it comes to cleaning and maintaining the pond, the rules for both the in-substrate pond and the self-contained pond are essentially the same. Obtain an aquarium siphon, and whenever the pond needs it, siphon out as much water as is necessary to clean the pond. The amount of water to be siphoned out and the degree of thoroughness with which you clean your pond will vary based on the conditions of its dirtiness. If, for example, you own a moderately sized Nile monitor, and it excreted its waste into a self-contained pond, you'll likely have to siphon out all of the water and wipe down the insides of the dish with a paper towel before refilling it with clean bottled water.

If, on the other hand, you've

Humid, not Wet

Standing pools of water will evaporate over time and can add water vapor to your tank. But if you need to maintain high humidity levels in your terrarium, consider adding an undertank heating pad to a corner of the terrarium. Set a water dish or bowl atop this pad; seat it deeply enough in the substrate that the heat from the undertank pad reaches it efficiently. As the water in the bowl warms, it will evaporate very quickly, adding a lot of water vapor into your tank in a very short period. You can fine-tune this humidity-adding device by adjusting the amount of substrate between the bottom of the water dish and the heating pad (the thicker the substrate, the slower the water evaporates) or by putting the heating pad on a timer so that the system only heats for predetermined and controlled durations. Species such as the mountain horned dragons (*Acanthosaura*), day geckos, (*Phelsuma*), and many amphibians will greatly benefit from such a setup.

established a liquid water table-style pond and you simply cannot see inside because of the algae growing on the inside of the glass, simply scrub the glass while the water is still in the pond, siphon out all the chunks of algae suspended in the water, and then refill until the water table line is 2 to 3 inches (5 to 7.6 cm) beneath the top of the substrate. The more plant life you have in your pond, the less often you'll have to siphon out and clean it, because the root systems of these plants can do wonders in keeping the water clean, the odor down, and the pond living and thriving as it would in the wild.

Moss (shown here with a Pacific giant salamander) will fare best if you use a misting or fogging system.

Making Rain

One benefit of the liquid water table pond that is not possible with the self-contained pond is the inclusion of a rain shower. Particularly valuable to hobbyists wishing to spur their pet frogs, toads, or salamanders into spawning behaviors, the rain shower is also an excellent way to water the mosses and shallow-growing plants in your terrarium. In addition, a rain shower inside the terrarium is physically and psychologically stimulating to a variety of temperate and tropical herp species. After all, you're going for as natural a feel in your tanks as you can get, and rainstorms are an important part of nature.

Begin setting up a rain shower in your terrarium by getting a powerful fully submersible aquarium filter or water pump. Sink this item in the pond of your terrarium, and attach a length of clear hose to the expulsion nozzle of the pump. The hose should fit snugly around the expulsion nozzle, because you'll need all the water pressure you can get. Run the other end of the hose up and out of the terrarium, and anchor it into a pre-drilled length (about 12 to 18 inches [30 to 46 cm] long) of PVC pipe. Make sure that the other end of the PVC pipe is tightly capped, and only drill about 18 to 24 tiny holes in just one side of the PVC pipe. If you drill holes in the other sides, you'll have tiny jets of water spraying in every direction when you turn on the pump.

Next, situate the drilled length of pipe atop the screen lid of the terrarium with the drilled side facing downward into the terrarium. Now plug in the submersible filter. If all your hoses are properly connected, the following should occur: the pump will begin taking in water from the liquid water table pond in your terrarium, the expulsion nozzle will pump the water up and out of your tank and into the drilled length of PVC pipe, and as the pipe fills with water, tiny jets of water will begin spraying out of the pipe and raining back down into your terrarium. The water will then soak back down through the substrate (watering any shallow-rooted plants as it goes) and right back into your pond. You've just created a miniature rain shower inside your naturalistic terrarium. Congratulations!

A word of caution is in order before constructing a rain shower in your terrarium. By virtue of the powerful pump you'll have to use, ensure that there are no aquatic herps in your terrarium that might be at risk of getting sucked into or up against the side of the aquarium pump. Ponds containing tadpoles, froglets, or other tiny or delicate animals are not suitable for the creation of a pump-driven rain shower.

Including a misting system in the terrarium will benefit many rainforest herps, such as red-eyed tree frogs.

Should you house a large herp or a colony of small herps, you must test the pH and overall quality of your pond water before you begin the rain shower. If the pH is lower than 6.4, if the ammonia level is high, or if the water smells foul or soiled, you must not conduct a rain shower. If it were pumped through the hose and made into a rain shower, pond water that is this degraded would prove extremely detrimental to the plant and animal life of your tank.

Remember, a natural rain is good, clean, pure water raining back down to the earth, so your artificial rain shower must be the same thing. If you are unsure about the quality of water in your pond, take the time to siphon the old water out and replace it with fresh, clean bottled water at least 24 hours before establishing a rain shower in your terrarium. Your animals and plants will thank you for taking the added precautions!

Chapter 7

Natural Terrarium Types

I like to think of this section as a sort of recipe book: It provides you a list of all the basic ingredients and a formula for mixing them together so that you can arrive at a well-balanced, fully functioning naturalistic terrarium. Like all good recipes, though, my descriptions are subject to variation. While I may suggest planting arrowhead and Mexican tree fern together in a cluster to provide shelter for small frogs or salamanders, you may find that a thick stand of devil's ivy works better within the confines of your own tank. That's one of the most beautiful aspects of building a naturalistic terrarium; as long as you follow the rules of nature, you can let your imagination be your guide.

Frog-eyed geckos (*Teratoscincus* spp.) fare very well in sandy desert terrariums if provided with a humidified hiding place.

Desert Terrariums

Let's start the recipe book off in the driest possible environment: the desert. Not all deserts are the same; some deserts, such as many of the ones in North America, are arid, rocky places that support a wide variety of plant life. Other deserts, such as those found in northern Africa, tend to be much sandier and largely devoid of plant life.

Because of the disparities between the sandy, dry, and plant-free environment of northern Africa and the rocky, heavily planted deserts of central Africa and North America, the hobbyist must decide which of these desert styles he will construct based on the herp species that will be housed in the terrarium. If the animal is native to the deserts of either North America or central Africa, it will not likely do well in the barren, sand-banked terrarium constructed in the style of northern Africa. The opposite is just as true, especially if you plan to house species adapted to burrow through loose sand, such as the sand boas. In a nutshell, the type of animal you own will govern whether you construct a rocky desert terrarium or a sandy desert terrarium.

Sandy Desert

Let's begin by constructing a sandy desert environment. Start by purchasing a long, low, wide terrarium because life in the desert landscape uses horizontal space, not vertical space. For this habitat style, a larger floor space is definitely preferable over vertical height. A tank sporting a sandy desert environment must be fitted with a screen lid that allows for maximum ventilation because there is no room for excess humidity buildup in this habitat type.

The sandy desert is a place of harsh winds, scorching heat, and a blazing sun that hangs like a fiery inferno in the sky. Life in this environment is extremely difficult, and the animals that call this place home have very special adaptations to help them cope with the shifting sands and raging heat of the sandy desert. Most notable among these adaptations, and a point that is of prime concern to the hobbyist interested in establishing a sandy desert

terrarium, is these animals' propensity for digging, burrowing, and tunneling under the sandy substrate. Many sandy desert-going animals travel, hunt, sleep, and hide all while keeping their entire body hidden beneath the sand. This subterranean lifestyle protects the herps from the scorching sun and allows them to stay concealed from would-be predators that scour the desert's surface in search of a meal.

Most inhabitants of sandy deserts are burrowers, such as the Kenyan sand boa.

While this may sound somewhat outlandish, sand-borrowing species will keep your terrarium in constant flux. You may anchor an item in the morning when you get up, only to find it turned over on its side and 2 inches (5 cm) deeper into the substrate by the time you get home in the evening. Flat stones and smaller decorative items, such as in-pot anchored succulents, that you place in your tank one evening, could easily be entirely sunken under the sands by the time you wake up in the morning. It's truly amazing how liquid-like the integrity of the sand is when populated by burrowing herps; your décor can sink under the sand and disappear almost as quickly as it would had you dropped it in a tank full of water.

So how do you conquer this shifting, sinking problem when decorating the sandy desert terrarium? You must seat any and all décor items on the base glass of the terrarium before adding any substrate. When your burrowing herps slide and slither through the sands that are directly beneath the décor items, the sand is briefly displaced, and the layer of sand above it falls down to fill in that displacement. As the herp continues to burrow, the décor item sinks lower and lower into the sand. When the décor item is already sitting as low as it can in the terrarium, the item cannot sink; thus, it will not be moved and shifted about in the terrarium.

The only downside to seating your décor items directly on the base glass of the terrarium is that you must find very large items to place there. You will have to purchase décor items that are at least 30 to 50 percent larger or longer than you might normally need for terrarium furnishings.

Décor What kind of décor does someone use for a sandy desert? I recommend using driftwood as your primary design element. Driftwood is fairly similar to the long-dead, sun-bleached limbs and branches that naturally occur along the fringes of the Sahara Desert, so they will look natural in your tank. Driftwood is also very utilitarian in this style of terrarium. Stand a piece up at an angle in the tank to create a climbing branch or basking spot for your herps. You also may wish to use stones for this purpose, but the driftwood is much lighter in weight than a comparably sized stone; thus, you run a much lower risk of cracking the base glass of your terrarium, which is a very real possibility when using a large stone. If you do use driftwood in your terrarium, make sure that it is untreated with any type of shellac or varnish. You want dry, clean, natural wood for this purpose.

Rocks also may be incorporated into the sandy desert terrarium, although they should be used sparingly. The type of rock you use is of little importance because the pH of the substrate will be pretty alkaline, and because you are severely limited in the plants you use, there is little concern of pH swing in the substrate. Use whatever rocks appeal to you and seem to look natural in the type of terrarium you are creating.

Sandblasted grapevines are often sold in pet stores and look quite natural in a desert terrarium.

Plants There are only a scant few plants that will work in the sandy desert terrarium. I personally favor the members of the *Euphorbia* genus. These thin, thorny plants do well in arid, tropical environments, although their need for intense sunlight can sometimes be problematic. Especially nice species include E. *decaryi*, E. *francoisii*, and E. *milloti*, all of which will do well when housed in the company of small reptiles or invertebrates. Large animals, such as the *Uromastyx* or other large agamids, should not be housed with any species of *Euphorbia* because these herbivorous and omnivorous lizards may nibble upon or even scratch open the *Euphorbia* plant, thus releasing its noxious latex. All members of the *Euphorbia* genus produce a thick, white, resinous latex that is harmful to the eyes, nostrils, and skin of any reptile that comes into contact with it. For this reason, members of the *Euphorbia* genus are best kept with only very small, strictly carnivorous herps. I recommend anchoring these plants in their own potting matrix using the in-pot method described in Chapter 5.

Top Ten: Desert Plants

1. *Notocactus leninghausii*
2. *Sansevieria t. hahnii*
3. *Sansevieria subspicata*
4. *Echinofossulocactus albatus*
5. *Opuntia microdasys*
6. *Lobivia aurea*
7. *Gymnocalycium mihanovichii*
8. *Sansevieria kirkii*
9. *Sansevieria trifasciata*
10. *Sansevieria patens*

Construction Begin construction of the sandy desert terrarium by seating your décor items directly on the base glass of the tank. Then stand a 4.5 inch (11 cm) tall length of half-inch (1.3 cm) PVC pipe (the length of the pipe may vary based on the depth of the substrate; a few inches [5 cm or so] need to protrude out of the substrate) in the back corner of the terrarium (explained later in this chapter). Make sure that the bottom of this pipe (the end that touches the glass) has several small holes drilled in it. Some hobbyists may wish to add a drainage layer of stones, although it has been my experience that few desert tanks benefit noticeably from a drainage layer. Now add silica-based sand to the tank until you have an even layer that is at least 3.5 inches (9 cm) deep. You can layer the sand much thicker than this, depending on the terrarium and which animals you plan to keep.

I recommend using only silica-based sand for this terrarium type because silica sand virtually never clumps together. Other sands, like limestone or sedimentary sands, for example, may clump together or form hard-packed layers through which no snake or lizard can easily burrow. Herp species, such as sandfish, that need to burrow rapidly need silica-based or granite-based sands that will allow them to easily "swim" through their subterranean world.

Cholla cactus skeletons make great decorations for desert terrariums. Most pet stores that carry herps will sell cholla.

Heating and Lighting Because sand is such a poor conductor of heat, heating a sandy desert terrarium can sometimes be a tricky issue. I recommend placing two or more (depending on how large your terrarium is) undertank heating pads on the bottom of the terrarium. These pads adhere to the bottom-outside of the tank and gently radiate warmth up through the substrate. Connect them (and your other heating devices) to a high-quality thermostat to keep terrarium temperatures in an acceptable range.

You also will need to provide heat from above. Ceramic heat emitters are a favorite of sandy desert hobbyists because they generate an astonishing amount of dry heat. Anyone who keeps plant life in his sandy desert terrarium may have to resort to high wattage lightbulbs, which will provide both heat for the herps and light for the vegetation. If you house desert species that must bask to metabolize calcium (most desert lizards fall into this category), you'll want to place a full-spectrum bulb atop the terrarium, including one that emits ultraviolet B waves.

Watering Just because the sandy desert is a very arid place does not mean that the herp species will not need water in some form. In the wild, these animals obtain much of the water they require from the foods they eat, but in captivity, keepers need to augment that water supply. This is where the PVC pipe sunken into the substrate comes into play. Once each week, it will be necessary to pour a quantity of water down that pipe to moisten the depths of the sandy substrate. One-half cup (118 ml) of water per every 2 square feet (0.2 square meter) of floor space will usually suffice. Use a humidity gauge to make sure that the humidity does not get too high.

There should be no standing water low in the tank, but the lowest depths of the tank must be moist. In the wild, moisture collects beneath the desert sands, so this aspect of the desert should be included in your naturalistic sandy desert terrarium. Depending on what species of herps you house, another method of providing water, such as a permanent water dish, may be necessary.

Rocky Desert

Wild rocky deserts are very different than their sandy counterparts, and hobbyists need to construct their own mini deserts according to those differences. Begin setting up your rocky desert terrarium by selecting a low, wide tank. Like the sandy desert, this biome type requires more floor space and less vertical height.

Substrate Compose a substrate mixture primarily of sand. Try to find a good, coarse sand, such as that found on a creek bank or river bank. Avoid play sand and any sand that is primarily limestone based, because these are very alkaline and may inhibit plant growth. A good sand for this terrarium style will be loose enough that any desert herps or invertebrates can dig permanent burrows and shelters in it (as they would in nature) but one that will also pack down and settle once it is in the terrarium.

Once you've found your sand, purchase some shredded or finely ground coconut husks, also known as coir. Moisten the coir and drain it. In a large bucket, mix the coir with the sand in the ratio of 1 part coir to 2 parts sand. I recommend adding about 1/4 cup (60 ml) of organic fertilizer and 1/4 cup (60 ml) of a trace mineral additive to every 2.5 gallons (9 l) of this mixture to benefit future plant growth. Mix thoroughly so that the fertilizers blend evenly into the mix. I call this substrate the desert "hard-pack" mixture, and it's worked great for me and other hobbyists for decades.

Unless you have very heavy items that need the added stability of being seated on the base glass of the terrarium, you'll want to add your hard-pack mixture into the terrarium before adding any plants or décor. Because many desert species, even small lizards, burrow extensively, it is always advisable to anchor all large décor on the base glass if you are unsure of the burrowing potential of your captives. An ounce of prevention is worth more than a pound of cure.

I recommend layering the hard-pack mixture at least 4 to 5 inches (10 to 13 cm) deep, depending on the size of your terrarium. The deeper your hard-pack mixture is, the better for any burrowing species of herps or inverts you may house, because in the wild, some species can construct deep, elaborate tunnels and burrows through the substrate.

Décor After layering your substrate mixture down, place your décor around the tank in such

Lighting Tip

In any desert terrarium, I recommend using a bulb that offers no less than 8 percent UV-A and UV-B rays. Leave this light on over your sun-worshipping herps for 12 to 14 hours each day. Your plants will appreciate the lights, too.

a way as to be both aesthetically pleasing and accommodating to the natural needs of your herps. Rocky structures need not be of any particular type or composition, but most natural deserts have a characteristic type of stone. Because your terrarium will not be receiving large amounts of water, the decay of the stones and the leaching of their mineral content into the

Rosy boas are one of the most recommended of the desert-dwelling reptiles.

substrate should not be a major concern. Granites, which are slow to decompose anyway, make a great addition to the tank, as do hunks of Mexican bowl lava and some types of slate or shale. Rocks mined from Arizona and Utah tend to have vibrant red and orange colors, and can add a definite touch of flare to your rocky desert terrarium. Petrified wood pieces, such as those found in Arizona, are interesting and quite natural looking.

I suggest searching through a rock yard or specialist pet shop when choosing your rocks. Secured rocky structures (avoid loosely stacking these rocks, lest they topple) such as caves and low mounds will be appreciated as basking sites by lizard species such as collared lizards, swifts, and whiptails (Cnemidophorus). Particularly skilled keepers—those who can meet its dietary need of tiny ants—might use the same setup to house a single or several horned lizards (Phrynosoma), although supplying them the ants they feed on may be difficult. Similarly, desert-going snake species, such as the rosy boas, Baird's rat snake, and most desert rattlesnakes, enjoy the feeling of comfort and security that comes with squeezing into a tight crevasse or gap in a rocky mound. Rocks of different heights also provide a vertical thermogradient that your herps will utilize.

Wood also has its place in the rocky desert terrarium. Dried lengths of driftwood—those that look gnarled, weathered, and sun bleached—give the best aesthetic appearance and make for some excellent structures. Sand-blasted grape vines and cork bark hollows also work nicely, the latter making great hiding places for the animals. Placed vertically or at an angle in the tank, this wood will act as a climb, while a horizontally placed slab of driftwood will be used by your herps as a hideaway.

Plants After your nonliving decorations are in place, you'll want to add some vegetation. When most of us think of desert plants, our minds immediately jump to images of tall cacti and short, stubby succulents. While these plants do exist in the rocky deserts of the American West, they are by no means the most common plant.

There are a great many succulents, shrubs, and woody-stemmed plants that will thrive in your hard-pack substrate. Some excellent varieties include *Sempervivum*, *Echeveria*, *Aloe*, *Sedum*, *Conophytum*, *Sansevieria*, *Fritha*, *Stapelia*, and *Hawthoria*. Truth be told, there are so many plant species that can successfully be cultivated within the rocky desert terrarium that an entire book could be written just on them. For our purposes here, however, I can only recommend that you spend the time and effort it takes to find the right plants for your tank. Take your time and choose the ones that are most pleasing to you and that pose absolutely no threat to your herps.

Avoid some excessively thorny cacti and some plants that ooze noxious resins. Because your terrarium is likely fairly short,

Some of the steps in constructing a rocky desert terrarium. 1.) Four inches (10 cm) of a 4:1 sand and coir substrate is placed in the terrarium. 2.) A few small potted cacti (*Notocactus sucineus* and *Theocactus conothelos*) are added with pots buried in the substrate. 3.) Some small rocks are added for shelters and basking sites. If you plan on housing burrowing or highly active species, it is best to seat the rocks on the very bottom of the terrarium.

Top Ten: Desert Reptiles

1. Rosy boa *(Lichanura trivirgata)*
2. Leopard gecko *(Eublepharis macularius)*
3. Schneider's skink *(Eumeces schneideri)*
4. Collared lizard *(Crotaphytus collaris)*
5. Kenyan sand boa *(Eryx colubrinus)*
6. Bearded dragon *(Pogona vitticeps)*
7. Uromastyx *(Uromastyx* ssp.*)*
8. Sandfish skink *(Scincus scincus)*
9. Egyptian tortoise *(Tesudo kleinmanni)*
10. Gray-banded kingsnake *(Lampropeltis alterna)*

The gecko and the Egyptian tortoise will require humidified hiding areas. Bearded dragons and uromastyx will try to eat most plants, so select the plants that you include with care.

avoid anchoring tall-growing plants in your mini desert. Flowering cacti, such as crassulas and kalanchoes, often produce long, flowing spikes (called "inflorescences") that may grow several inches (15 cm or so) taller than the cactus itself. You don't want these flowering spikes to outgrow the height of the tank. Remember not to go overboard when adding vegetation to the rocky desert terrarium. Too many plants can raise the relative humidity in the tank to unacceptably high levels, which can cause all sorts of problems in the desert environment.

Water your rocky desert terrarium very sparingly. Most succulent plant species will have shallow roots, so the most efficient way to water them is to squirt a small stream of water from a handheld spray bottle directly around the base of the plant. You must never water the entire substrate of the rocky desert terrarium. Because they are so well adapted to life amid the dryness of rocks and sand, these plants need only be watered every eight to ten days, depending on the exact species in question. I heard a phrase once about watering the desert terrarium that has always stuck with me: "Wait ten, then do it again!" Water your rocky desert terrarium plants, wait ten days, then water each plant again. I've kept rocky desert terrariums off and on for years, and I've found that this method of watering works very well.

Heating and Lighting Lighting and heating of the rocky desert terrarium will depend largely on the needs of the herps and the plants you house inside. Most rocky desert terraria do well with 12 to 14 hours of full spectrum lighting that emits both UV-A and UV-B rays. I recommend a bulb that emits 8 percent or higher UV-B rays.

Create a basking area by placing an incandescent spotlight over one end of the tank. Have a stack of rocks or a slanted length of driftwood directly beneath this light so that your herps can climb up and get that much closer to the source of heat and light. As a general rule of thumb, a rocky desert terrarium that houses diurnal lizards will need to be the best lit because these sun-worshipping animals require intense levels of light and heat if they are to thrive.

I recommend a basking spot that reaches 90° to 95°F (32.2° to 35°C). Most desert snakes and nocturnal lizards, on the other hand, do not need such intense lighting or heat. These animals may be maintained with only moderate light levels—enough to simulate a day/night cycle and accommodate viewing of the tank is best. Your plants also may require more or less intense levels of light. When selecting plants for your terrarium, keep light requirements in mind because if you anchor a mismatched hodgepodge of succulents in your terrarium, you risk denying the light-loving species ample lighting or giving too much light to the shade-loving species.

Savanna Terrarium

Semi-arid but more heavily planted than either of the desert styles, the savanna represents the transition between desert land and forest. The air is dry, but the annual rainfall in the savanna is much higher than in the desert, and the soil is neither a sandy nor a hard-pack substrate. It is a border land between biomes, and it is constantly in flux. Vegetation comes and goes with the seasons on the savanna, and in the home terrarium, some species of aging or dying plants occasionally may have to be replaced with fresh, vigorous specimens.

Opuntia macrodasys, commonly called bunny ears cactus, often does well in desert terrariums if it is placed near a bright light. Its soft spines cannot injure most herps.

The savanna is a biome that is highly suited to a wide variety of large lizard species, such as the monitors and the bearded dragon. A plethora of equatorial African snakes also call the savanna home, such as pythons, vipers, and numerous colubrids.

Enclosure

Construct the savanna terrarium by selecting a tank that is wide and long, with some height to it—perhaps 18 inches (46 cm) tall. Most species of savanna-dwelling herps will require large floor space, although some monitor lizards or snakes also may require elevated climbing branches. If you intend to house an arboreal species, select a tank that is both tall and offers plenty of floor space.

Terrarium Parameters

The below table is a breakdown of the basic physical parameters of our naturalistic terrarium types. Remember that these numbers are just guidelines; each parameter is dependent on the species you are keeping.

Terrarium Type	Temperature Range	Relative Humidity	Air Circulation	Inhabitant Types
Sandy Desert	80°-110° (26-43°C)	< 50%	High	Reptiles, Invertebrates
Rocky Desert	80°-100° (26-38°C)	< 50%	High	Reptiles, Invertebrates
Savanna	75°-95° (23-35°C)	50%-60%	High	Reptiles, Invertebrates
Montane	70°-85° (21-29°C)	60%-75%	Moderate	Reptiles, Amphibians, Invertebrates
Jungle	80°-100° (26-38°C)	70%-85%	Moderate	Reptiles, Amphibians, Invertebrates
Semi-Aquatic	75°-100° (23-38°C)	70%-85%	Moderate	Reptiles, Amphibians

Substrate

Of the terrarium types we've seen thus far, this is the first style in which I recommend placing a shallow layer of aquarium pebbles in the bottom of the tank to aid in drainage purposes. The savanna terrarium normally doesn't require enough moisture to warrant such drainage, but some species of monitors require more moisture than other species, and some species of plants used in the savanna terrarium may take more water than others. It's better to have the layer of pebbles in the tank and never need them than it is to need this drainage layer and it not be there. This layer need not exceed 1.5 inches (3.8 cm) in depth.

The next layer to place down is a 1 to 1.5 inch (2.5 to 3.8 cm) thick layer of composting leaves. These leaves must stay fairly low in the substrate mix because you'll need their beneficial bacteria and fungi, but if the layer is too shallow in the tank, they will dry out and their fungi will die off. As the roots of your plants grow down through this layer of

Small snakes from the central and western US, longnose snakes (*Rhinocheilus lecontei*) are good subjects for a rocky desert terrarium, but they often insist on eating lizards.

composting leaves, the plants will enjoy all the benefits of a fertile, biologically active growing media, but the upper levels of the mixture will remain amply dry.

Once the pebbles and composting leaf layers are down, concoct a substrate mix that is 1 part nonsilica sand and 2 parts moist coconut husk (coir). Into this mixture, add about 1/4 cup (60 ml) of both organic fertilizer and a trace mineral additive to ensure the slow release of ample nutrients into the substrate. Depending on the burrowing needs of your herp or invertebrate species, you may want to layer this substrate deeper or shallower. Monitors and tortoises may require deeper substrata, while geckos and many snake species won't care about the depth of the substrate.

Décor

After placing your substrate, consider décor. Again, driftwood is probably your best option, as are slabs of bark, large stones or rocky outcroppings, and the skeletons of dead cacti, which add a unique flare to any savanna terrarium.

When it comes to placing stones in the savanna terrarium, use those varieties that look natural but that will not leach calcium or sodium into the environment. It's okay to use calcium- or sodium-rich stones (such as limestone) in this style of terrarium as long as you do not pour copious amounts of water directly over these stones or even into the substrate immediately surrounding them. Red slates and other vibrantly colored (some of the best come from Australia, Utah, or Arizona) stones are some of the most attractive stones that can be employed in the savanna terrarium.

Plants

Use seedling acacias and clumping species of grasses because natural savannas are renowned for their endless, rolling fields and hills of lush grass. Bermuda grass (*Cynodon dactylon*) is an excellent species to use under intense lighting conditions because it will send runners throughout the substrate and eventually populate virtually the entire tank. Summer wheat grass is another fine plant because it provides excellent cover for grass-loving species.

The major drawback to using grasses in the home terrarium is the frequency with which they must be replaced. Most grasses that are suitable to life in the terrarium are short-lived species that need to be dug out and replaced annually. This makes the savanna terrarium the most maintenance-intensive and challenging style of terrarium.

Other plants are also suitable for the savanna terrarium. Shrubs and woody-stemmed plants, such as juniper, caudexed figs, ponytail palms, and various species of *Euphorbia* and *Sansevieria* make excellent long-term additions to the terrarium. If trimmed back each season, juniper makes a fabulous plant for the savanna biome because it provides cover, shade, and a climbing venue for a host of small lizard and snake species, as well as granting a shedding rub for snakes. Juniper is also a highly attractive plant species. If trimmed like a bonsai, a couple of juniper shrubs can give your savanna terrarium an ancient, rugged appearance. In addition, juniper is virtually impossible to kill in the home terrarium. Any hobbyist interested in constructing a savanna terrarium should consider using some species of juniper, especially a dwarf cultivar.

By virtue of the short-lived nature of the grasses suitable for use in the savanna terrarium, many hobbyists prefer to use the in-pot method of planting. They feel that when the plants need replacing, their task of digging them up and replacing them with fresh plants is much easier. Perhaps it is, but I've found that such grasses usually live longer if they are anchored directly into the substrate. If left in their pots, these plants will not send an ample number of their roots deep into the composting leaf layer of the substrate; thus, they will not reap the nutrient benefits found therein. Likewise, many small monitor species and other savanna-going lizards enjoy burrowing directly beneath the root systems of these grasses. In the wild, the root systems provide cool shelter for the lizard, and they attract both insect and rodent prey on which the lizard feeds. This is why it is best to anchor your plants using the in-substrate method of planting.

There are several species of armadillo lizards that will thrive in a savanna or rocky desert terrarium. *Cordylus cataphractus* is a fairly common species.

Monitors and Grass

By planting tall grasses in the savanna terrarium, the hobbyist may be able to witness the remarkable hunting behaviors of various monitor species. In the wild, several species of monitor lizards often hunt among tall grasses, including argus monitors and savanna monitors. To spot their prey, these carnivorous lizards stand on their hind legs, using their tail as a third prop, and peer out over the grasses. Under normal captive conditions, this is seldom seen, but in a spacious (i.e., room-sized) savanna terrarium, it can become a commonplace behavior.

Water the savanna terrarium every five to eight days, depending on the watering needs of the plants you have chosen. As is the case in the rocky desert terrarium, water only very close to the root systems of your plants; do not saturate the substrate.

Heating and Lighting

Heating and lighting can be applied in much the same manner as described for the rocky desert-style terrarium. An ultraviolet light is mandatory, and an additional heating lamp or ceramic heat emitter also may be needed, depending on the needs of your herps. Days are long on the savanna, so leave the lights on for 12 to 14 hours a day during the summer months and 8 to 10 hours during the winter.

Woodland Terrarium

Fourth on the list of terrarium types is the woodland or temperate forest. Characterized by moderate levels of humidity, rich and fertile soil, and plenty of low-growing vegetation, the woodland terrarium can host a very wide variety of herps and invertebrates from all over the world. The plant life that will thrive in the woodland terrarium is also highly diverse. There is so much room for diversity when it comes to constructing the woodland terrarium, in fact, that it is very rare to see two woodland tanks that look alike.

Enclosure

Begin constructing a woodland terrarium by selecting an appropriately sized terrarium. Unlike the desert styles discussed so far, the woodland terrarium usually requires a considerable measure of height—no less than 24 inches (61 cm) tall—because such height

Top Ten: Reptiles of the Savanna

1. **Western hognose snake** *(Heterodon nasicus)*
2. **Long-tailed grass lizard** *(Takydromus sexlineatus)*
3. **Great Plains rat snake** *(Pantherophis emoryi)*
4. **Western plains garter snake** *(Thamnophis radix haydeni)*
5. **Baird's rat snake** *(Pantherophis obsoletus bairdi)*
6. **Armadillo lizard** *(Cordylus cataphractus)*
7. **Ball python** *(Pythons regius)*
8. **Fence lizard** *(Sceloporus undulatus)*
9. **Moorish gecko** *(Tarentola mauritanica)*
10. **African house snakes** *(Lamprophis spp.)*

The Moorish gecko and armadillo lizard also will thrive in a rocky desert terrarium.

will be necessary to accommodate both the climbing branches required by arboreal herp species and the long-term growth of some of the taller plants. Because the level of humidity in the woodland tank needs to be relatively high with ample ventilation, use both a wire mesh screen lid and impermeable glass or an acrylic lid. Covering the entire top of the tank with a screen lid will allow for ample ventilation and prevent your herps from escaping; topping this off with an acrylic or glass lid that covers roughly half of the tank's top will help to trap enough moisture inside the terrarium to maintain an appropriate level of relative humidity. If in doubt, use a humidity gauge to monitor the relative humidity in the tank, and make sure that it isn't too high or too low for the animals.

Substrate

After selecting the terrarium, compose a substrate mixture. I've found that a good recipe for woodland substrate consists of the following: 1 part ground palm bark, 1 part ground or shredded coconut husks, 1 part orchid bark, and 2 parts composting leaf litter. This mixture makes an excellent substrate. It drains well but is moisture retentive enough to support a wide variety of plant life. It's very lightweight and of neutral or only slightly acidic pH, which benefits the root systems of a wide range of plant species. The composting leaves grant the mixture a high level of biological activity. As you create the mixture, mix in 1.5 tablespoons of broad spectrum organic fertilizer and 2 tablespoons of organic nitrogen supplement fertilizer (such as blood meal) per 2 gallons (7.5 l) of substrate mix.

Before layering in the substrate mix, place a 1.5- to 2-inch-deep (3.8- to 5-cm-deep) layer of aquarium gravel in the bottom of the tank to accommodate drainage. Layer the substrate fairly thick atop these stones; I suggest 4 to 5 inches (10 to 13 cm) as the minimum depth. Unlike the desert terrariums, this substrate will be quite stable, and there is little chance of it shifting or sliding unless you plan to house a powerful burrowing species of herp. A depth of 4 to 5 inches (10 to 13 cm) will allow most plant species (even very tall ones) to get a firm grip in the soil.

Plants

The good news about plants in this terrarium is that there is a huge variety from which to select. Just take a trip to your local nursery or greenhouse, and select any species that will thrive within a temperate habitat. Ferns and ivies make excellent ground cover; appropriate taller varieties of foliage include arrowhead, *Aralia*, and some species of *Philodendron*, *Peperomia*, and *Fatsia*.

Because of the permanence of the substrate layer within the woodland terrarium, use in-substrate planting methods. If you have a young or delicate plant (a cutting or newly rooted specimen), anchor it in-pot style in a biodegradable pot that will soon decompose.

Ground Cover

Once you have the substrate down and your plants in place, it's time to consider what type of ground cover you will use. Ground cover is an essential component in the woodland, jungle, and swamp terrariums but is unnecessary in the rocky and sandy desert-style terrariums. Any terrarium in which the soil must maintain a high degree of moisture must be supplied with some type of ground cover to prevent the substrate mix from drying out too quickly.

Several species of invertebrates will do well in a savanna terrarium, including the red-kneed tarantula (*Brachypelma smithi*).

In the woodland-style tank, place a layer of tropical moss or a dense layer of composting leaves atop the substrate. The moss, which will grow into a thick carpet over the floor of the terrarium in time, is very efficient at retaining moisture within the substrate. If you are not skilled enough yet to cultivate a carpet of moss (or if you house a large herp that will crush or destroy a moss layer), a layer of composting leaves left atop the substrate also will do a pretty good job of keeping the substrate adequately moist. Layer this ground cover especially thick around the base of any tall plants within the tank because this will ensure that their root systems stay amply moist at all times.

Décor

With the ground cover of your terrarium in place, it's time to establish the rest of the tank's décor. The décor of the woodland tank is a little bit trickier than any terrarium discussed so far. By virtue of the moderate levels of humidity in the woodland tank, any stones placed in it are subject to decomposition and leaching. Avoid using organic limestone or other loose, chalky stones because these will rapidly decompose in the semi-moist environment of the woodland tank, leaching their mineral content into the soil and drastically raising the pH of the substrate. Few woodland plant species can tolerate substrate that has an overly high pH.

Igneous rocks will work in a woodland tank, altthough they will not appear very "natural" in such an environment. Metamorphic rocks, such as granite, are probably the hobbyist's best bet in the

Some of the steps in constructing a woodland terrarium. 1.) A substrate of coir and leaf litter is placed above a drainage layer of pea gravel. 2.) Leaf litter is placed on top of the substrate as a ground cover. 3.) Plants are added using in-substrate planting. The plants for this terrarium are an English ivy and some deciduous moss.

woodland tank. They naturally occur in woods and temperate forests, they are very resilient to leaching and breakdown, and they will not adversely affect the plants or herps of your terrarium.

Take similar precautions when selecting wooden structures to place in the woodland terrarium. Most types of wood are subject to deterioration and fungal colonization, especially those wooden items that have one end anchored in the moist substrate. Bear in mind that these activities are perfectly natural and can be beneficial, but when the ecological balance swings out of alignment in an enclosed terrarium, fungal explosions can occur.

If you plan to use lots of wooden décor in your tank, consider adding a higher ratio (3 parts) of decomposing leaf litter into the initial substrate mixture. This will ensure that the beneficial bacteria and fungi will be omnipresent throughout the mixture and will minimize the threat of a detrimental fungal or bacterial outbreak within the terrarium. A tank that has a relatively high density (more than 40 percent floor coverage) of plants is also less likely to suffer from an imbalance of fungal or bacterial activity on wooden décor items.

The Trouble With Moss

One of the only temperate plant types that I do not recommend using in the woodland terrarium is any species of temperate moss. While the moss we see in the woods is lush, green, and vibrant, it is only so because of its dormancy period the previous winter. Temperate mosses must have a period of dark and cool (as provided by a natural winter) if they are to reemerge and flourish the next year. Because you cannot easily simulate this in the home terrarium, temperate moss species will not last long in the naturalistic terrarium. Instead, use a tropical species of moss, which requires no such "downtime" to thrive. Although they are certainly not from the same natural plant community as your temperate plant species, the tropical and subtropical mosses will be full and flush year-round in the home naturalistic terrarium.

Heating and Lighting

Because the substrate of the woodland terrarium is so dense, undertank heating apparatus are virtually useless, and if employed, will lead to rapid moisture evaporation from the depths of the substrate. Heat and light your woodland tank with florescent or incandescent fixtures suspended above the terrarium.

Most woodland-dwelling herp species do not require nearly the amount of UV radiation that

A woodland terrarium housing house geckos and brown anoles. The plants include a philodendron, an ivy, and Christmas fern. Although an artificial feature, the fencing makes this terrarium unique.

Top Ten: Woodland Herps

1. **Green anole (*Anolis carolinensis*)**
2. **American toad (*Bufo americanus*)**
3. **Eastern box turtle (*Terrapene carolinenesis*)**
4. **Green tree frog (*Hyla cinerea*)**
5. **Rough green snake (*Opheodrys aestivus*)**
6. **Ruin lizard (*Podarcis sicula*)**
7. **House gecko (*Hemidactylus* ssp.)**
8. **African forest skinks (*Mabuya* ssp.)**
9. **Glass lizard (*Ophisaurus ventralis*)**
10. **Eastern milk snake (*Lampropeltis t. triangulum*)**

desert-going herps do, so you will not need to purchase such UV-intense bulbs. Some woodland species, particularly diurnal lizard species, do require some degree of UV radiation, however, so a full-spectrum bulb that emits UV-B waves might be necessary. Do your homework and find out what the lighting requirements of your herp species are before purchasing your fixture.

As they occur in nature, low-growing woodland plants naturally thrive on the cool, shady, forest floor; thus, their need for direct sunlight is low to moderate. Most temperate plants require this shade because the cellular structure of their leaves and stems will break down when subjected to intense light or heat (the human equivalent of getting a bad sunburn). If your lighting apparatus is too bright or too hot, your forest plants will rapidly wilt or scorch.

Jungle Terrarium

The next type of naturalistic terrarium on the docket is, in my estimation, the most popular style of terrarium going: the jungle. Sometimes referred to as the tropical forest style, the jungle terrarium is very similar to the woodland style in the setup and construction of the substrate mixture, although its heat, lighting, and moisture requirements are somewhat different.

Green tree frogs are recommended for the woodland terrarium. They are compatible with other small frogs and lizards, such as anoles, geckos, and skinks.

Enclosure

Easily the polar opposite of the desert-style terrarium, the jungle biome typically requires a very tall tank in which to thrive. I suggest using nothing shorter than 24 to 30 inches (61 to 76 cm) to accommodate sufficient plant growth and vertical habitat construction. Many available jungle-going herps and invertebrates are arboreal or semi-arboreal, and if housed in a terrarium that denies them the opportunity to climb and venture upward, these animals will severely stress and may contract stress-related ailments. Arboreal boas, pythons, colubrids, tree frogs, and lizard species must have plenty of vertical space if they are to thrive. The taller a terrarium you provide for your jungle habitat, the better for all plant and arboreal animal species involved.

Substrate

After selecting an amply tall terrarium, place a 1- to 2-inch (2.5- to 5-cm) layer of aquarium gravel in the bottom of the tank to serve as a drainage reservoir should you accidentally overwater the terrarium. Atop this gravel layer a 4- to 6-inch-deep (10- to 15-cm-deep) layer of substrate mixture. A suitable mix for the jungle habitat consists of 1 part coir (or ground coconut husks), 2 parts orchid bark, 2 parts composting leaves, and 1 part ground

A tall jungle terrarium housing emerald tree boas (*Corallus caninus*). Note the horizontal perches, which are needed for this species.

palm. As with the woodland mixture, augment this mixture with 2 tablespoons of organic, general-purpose fertilizer and 2 tablespoons of additional trace elements to help to kick-start the biological processes within the substrate.

Décor

Utilizing rocks in the jungle terrarium can be a tricky matter. As you already know, some types of rocks easily break down when subjected to perpetually moist conditions. All manner of sedimentary stones *must be avoided* in the jungle terrarium. If you must employ rocks in the jungle habitat, use Mexican lava rock or something of similar composition. You will find, however, that in most basic jungle habitats, there is little room for stones and rocky fixtures. Most hobbyists who build them are more interested in the plant life associated with the jungle, so they do not miss the stones anyway. In more advanced jungle habitats, however, many hobbyists successfully employ various types of igneous and metamorphic stones in elaborate jungle ponds and fern-banked streams flowing through their terrariums.

Plants

When it comes to adding plants and décor to the jungle terrarium, the sky's the limit. Orchids, African violets, and bromeliads are especially popular, but there are many species and cultivars from which to choose. I could easily take up an entire book discussing the various cultivars of bromeliads, orchids, and other jungle plants suitable for this terrarium type. A short list of plants includes copperleafs (*Acalypha*), elephant ears (*Alocasia*), carpet plants (*Episcia*), *Fittonia*, prayer plants (*Maranta*), and devil's ivy. Not all plants will live in all terrariums, so research which plants will do well under your specific conditions.

When anchoring your plants in the jungle terrarium, pack them in at a relatively low density at first, then add new specimens every few weeks until your terrarium is filled to capacity. It seems that within the jungle terrarium, there is always room for one more little plant to be tucked into this corner or that crevasse, so take your time and exercise some artistic license in creatively planting your jungle terrarium.

Of course, not all plants have to be anchored in the substrate of the tank. Unlike the terrarium types discussed so far, the jungle terrarium lends itself to vertical eco-planting. Bromeliads, by virtue of their not needing a root system, may be placed high in a moist nook of a climbing limb or anchored in a hollow within a taller plant. Commercially manufactured "coco-board" (a porous board made from compressed coconut husks) can be cut to fit and glued to the sides and back of your jungle terrarium. (Silicon aquarium sealant works well for securing the board to the glass wall of the tank.) Simply keep the boards moderately moist, and any bromeliads or penthouse orchids anchored in them will thrive without a problem. While not overly

Some of the steps in constructing a jungle terrarium. 1.) Place several inches (10 cm or so) of pea gravel on the bottom for drainage. 2.) Add several inches (10 cm) of a suitable substrate for plant growth, such as a mix of coir, peat, and leaf litter. 3.) Add the desired plants. Placing the plants in several clumps mimics nature and provides herp hiding places.

The author created this jungle terrarium to house a breeding colony of poison dart frogs in the ecology building of the University of Georgia.

attractive when the tank is initially established, these organic boards will play host to scores of tiny plants and mosses, and as the tank matures, the board will develop into a living, thriving wall of vegetation that is aesthetically pleasing.

Truth be told, it's pretty hard to overdo the amount of vegetation you have in your jungle terrarium. As long as there is ample moisture, light, and nutrients to support a dense community of plants, you should have no problem maintaining a thick, lush jungle habitat. One problem that many hobbyists do encounter, however, is that they get so carried away with adding plant life to their tank that they have to search every day to locate their pet herps hiding amidst such dense foliage. Remember to leave space for whatever species of animals you are keeping to move about and engage in normal behaviors.

Bear in mind that such thick, rich stands of vegetation will require that additional fertilizers be added every so often. In my 55-gallon (208-l) tank that I've liberally planted with various jungle plants, I like to add 1 teaspoon of nitrogenous fertilizer (a liquid variety mixed with cool, clear water) into the substrate every two months. I put this mixture in a garden sprayer and spray the substrate near the roots of the plants, and I notice an increase in growth rate and general beauty of my plants within a few days.

Ground Cover

As is true of the woodland terrarium, the jungle habitat must have a dense layering of some variety of ground cover to prevent the depths of the substrate from drying out due to evaporation. Some of the best ground cover is a carpet of some species of tropical or subtropical moss, such as *Vesicularia dubyana* or *Dicranum*, which thrives in lower Florida and points south, and it's readily available in the terrarium trade. Other good ground cover includes partially composted leaves that will dry on top but that will remain moist lower down. Anyone who has ever been to the jungles of Central or South America will attest to the thick covering of leaves on the jungle floor. Thus, utilizing a thick ground covering of leaves (avoid evergreen needles and magnolia leaves, which contain potentially harmful resins) in the jungle terrarium is a very naturalistic and realistic way to preserve the moisture within the depths of the substrate.

Pretty and strange, prayer plants (*Maranta tricolor*) need warm temperatures and high humidity, so they tend to do well in jungle terrariums.

Many jungle-dwelling herps will appreciate this leaf cover as well. Lizards, such as knight anoles and tegus, will hunt amidst this roughage, while leaf-tailed geckos will take great mental comfort in knowing that they are impeccably camouflaged against such a mottled backdrop. Some species of jungle frogs, such as mantellas and dendrobatids, may even be coaxed into depositing their eggs in water collected in the cup-like dish of an upturned fallen leaf.

Humidity

The animals and plants that naturally dwell in the rainforest require high levels of relative humidity to thrive. Maintain a relative humidity of no less than 75 percent and not more than 85 percent.

It is important to understand that not only is humidity important to the long-term health of your herps, but clean air and air circulation are critical to them as well. Stagnant air and tainted humidity are leading causes of infection and poor health in the jungle

Flying geckos are interesting subjects for the jungle terrarium. As with most other lizards, keep only one male per enclosure.

terrarium. Maintain a balance between high humidity and air circulation in your terrarium by checking and adjusting the humidity level daily. If the relative humidity has dipped below 72 to 75 percent, lightly mist the inside of the tank with a garden spray bottle and cover two-thirds of the tank's screen lid with glass or acrylic that will trap evaporating water vapor inside the terrarium. When the opposite scenario occurs and the air within your jungle terrarium becomes stale and smelly, partially remove the impermeable lid to allow more ventilation. Relative humidity is easily measured by way of a humidity gauge, which you can purchase from virtually any pet shop that deals in herps and herp products.

Heating and Lighting

Lighting your jungle terrarium is best done with the use of some type of florescent fixture. Grow lights, such as the type used in indoor greenhouses or enclosed botanical gardens, are best for this purpose. I advise using florescent fixtures for several reasons. First, the amount of heat produced by a florescent fixture is exponentially less than the amount of raw heat produced by an incandescent bulb. Tall plants and arboreal herps, both of which naturally thrive at the upper reaches of the tank, are particularly at risk when an incandescent bulb is used. Plants risk scorching, and arboreal herps will seek refuge by resting on the cooler floor of the tank—a behavior that is unnatural and very stressful for them. If you notice your arboreal herps spending an inordinate amount of time on the substrate, you'll want to lower the intensity of your lighting; either use fewer bulbs or use bulbs of lower wattage.

A second reason that I tout florescent lightbulbs is the amount of light they broadcast to your living plants. These bulbs are long and project even amounts of light to all points of the terrarium, especially when coupled with a reflector hood.

A final reason that I recommend using florescent bulbs over incandescent ones is the cost involved in their purchase and operation. On average, a florescent bulb has a life span of many times that of an incandescent bulb. A hobbyist lighting his tank with incandescent fixtures might have to replace these bulbs ten times before the hobbyist lighting his jungle tank with florescent bulbs has to replace his fixtures once. Similarly, the electricity used to power an incandescent bulb is much greater than that used for a florescent fixture.

Some jungle-living herps—notably chameleons, anoles, and other diurnal lizards—may require UV-B lighting. A plant grow light will not supply this type of radiation. Fortunately, full-spectrum lights that supply ultraviolet light for herps are good for plants. Be sure that you know the lighting requirements of your plants *and* your animals before you purchase the wrong types of bulbs.

As far as heat goes in the jungle terrarium, ample heat may or may not be admitted into the tank by your lighting apparatus. Some styles of terrarium hoods have multiple light fixtures mounted in them such that the main source of light may be broadcast by way of a florescent bulb, while auxiliary heat is emitted by low-wattage incandescent bulbs. This style of hood is highly recommended for use in the jungle-style terrarium. Simply fit an ample number of low-wattage incandescent bulbs into the proper fixtures, and monitor the heat inside your jungle terrarium by way of digital thermometers placed in at least two places—one near the lights and one as far away from the lights as possible. This placement allows you to see the complete range of temperatures present in your terrarium. If the temperature runs too high for your plant and animal life, lower the wattage of the bulbs used, or simply fit your hood with fewer bulbs. Conversely, if the temperature is too low for your plants and animals to thrive, you'll need to add bulbs or increase the wattage.

Line and Vine

I've seen hobbyists construct stunning vine-clad habitats through the creative use of fishing line. Virtually invisible when the terrarium is viewed from a distance, fishing line can be strung between two or more items within the terrarium to create a climbing venue for vining plants such as various species of ivy. Simply anchor a small ivy or vine plant near the lower end of the fishing line and watch as it slowly snakes its way upward to the top of your terrarium. Arboreal frogs, geckos, and anoles seem particularly fond of sheltering in and hunting amidst such vertical foliage.

Montane Terrarium

Another humid forest environment is one that few people really know a lot about, but it is one that I feel bears mentioning: the montane terrarium. The montane, or mountain-like,

Top Ten: Jungle Inhabitants

1. Tokay gecko *(Gekko gecko)*
2. Argentine horned frog *(Ceratophrys ornata)*
3. Crested gecko *(Rhacodactylus ciliatus)*
4. Red-eyed tree frog *(Agalychnis callidryas)*
5. Timor monitor *(Varanus timorensis)*
6. Knight anole *(Anolis equestris)*
7. Cuban tree frog *(Osteopilus septentriolalis)*
8. Giant day gecko *(Phelsuma madagascariensis grandis)*
9. Flying gecko *(Ptyochozoon spp.)*
10. Poison arrow frogs *(Dendrobates spp.)*

habitat is defined by its dense foliage, high levels of relative humidity, and relatively cool temperatures. It is a high-altitude environment in which a surprisingly large number of herp species can thrive. North American and European salamanders in particular relish the cool, moist montane environment, and even some snake species such as the Mandarin rat snake, the demure Chinese rat snake, and the green trinket snake do very well when housed in a montane terrarium.

Enclosure

Begin establishing your montane terrarium by selecting an enclosure. Montane habitats support tall plants and cool canopies, so height is definitely a factor to consider, but width and length are also important to establishing a thermocline inside the terrarium. For these reasons, most hobbyists constructing a montane environment opt for tall, long tanks, usually 100 gallons (379 l) or larger. Remember that bigger is almost always better when it comes to building a natural terrarium.

Unlike most geckos which are nocturnal, day geckos are active during the day, making them favorites in the jungle terrarium. A lined day gecko *(Phelsuma lineata)* is shown here.

Night Temps

For heating any type of terrarium at night, you can use red or blue lights, often sold as "moonglow" bulbs. This type of light will not disturb your herps' day–night cycle but will help to keep the temperature in the acceptable range. Constructed out of black, red, or dark purple glass, these bulbs will supply gentle, even warmth to your terrarium while bathing the habitat in a pale, soft glow. Another option is ceramic heat emitters, which produce heat without producing light. Bear in mind that some temperature drop at night is natural and acceptable within most terrarium types. Below is a short list showing suggested temperature drops at night. Remember to research the species you are keeping to find out exactly how much of a cooling that species prefers.

Desert: 8°–12°F (4.5°–6.7°C)	Jungle: 5°–7°F (2.7°–3.9°C)
Temperate Woodland: 5°–10°F (2.7°–5.6°C)	Montane: 10°-15°F (5.6°–8.3°C)
	Swamp: 5°–10°F (2.7°–5.6°C)

Substrate

Once you have the tank situated in your home, begin mixing your substrate in the same manner as recommended for the forest or woodland habitat: 1 part ground palm bark (or peat, if your chosen species of plants can tolerate the acidity), 1 part ground or shredded coconut husks, 1 part orchid bark, and 2 to 3 parts composting leaf litter. While the montane habitat and its inhabitants can vary significantly from the woodland habitat in terms of temperature, humidity, and lighting, the same biological activities that occur within the substrate of the woodland habitat also must transpire in the subterranean layers of the montane terrarium. In terms of maintaining a terrarium, there is no appreciable difference in soil types between these two biomes. Similarly, your montane habitat also will require the same 1- to 2-inch-thick (2.5- to 5-cm-thick) drainage layer at the bottom of the terrarium. Construct this layer using washed and rinsed pea gravel. The substrate above the drainage layer should be 3 to 5 inches (7.6 to 12.7 cm) deep.

Ground Cover

After layering in your drainage pebbles and substrate, place a generous layer of ground cover atop the substrate. Bear in mind that your montane substrate will likely need to retain more moisture than does a woodland tank, so a thicker ground covering is in order. Use temperate mosses (which may have to be replaced annually) or semi-tropical mosses that can survive in a cooler montane environment. A dense layer of surface leaf litter also will suffice.

Plants

Virtually all plants that will thrive in the temperate woodland terrarium also will thrive in the montane terrarium because most forest plants have more tolerance for temperature variations than do the woodland herps. Some of my favorite plants that work well in the montane habitat include the philodendrons, all species of the genus *Martana*, and ferns of the genera *Aglaomopha*, *Blechnum*, *Cibotium*, *Asplenium*, and *Nephrolepis*. Plant your montane terrarium as per the methods described for the jungle habitat, making sure not to overcrowd your tank and to leave plenty of room between plants for growth. Philodendron runners and excessively long fern fronds may require regular trimming.

Décor

Decorate using various driftwood and metamorphic or igneous stones. Avoid using sedimentary rocks due to the high humidity in the montane environment. Most montane-dwelling herp species are by nature quite shy and retiring, so make sure that you outfit your montane habitat with plenty of deep, dark hides.

Water and Humidity

The montane environments hobbyists usually seek to duplicate do not lack numerous sources of water; these habitats have springs, creeks, streams, ponds, and quiet pools to which the resident herps regularly travel to drink or hunt prey. Keep at least two large water dishes (or in-container-style ponds) for every 40 gallons (151 l) of terrarium space. A 125-gallon (473-l) tank, therefore, should contain three large water dishes situated throughout the terrarium.

Live moss looks very natural in a montane terrarium and makes a good ground cover.

If you keep your montane terrarium's temperatures cool to moderate, fire salamanders should be happy there.

Not only do so many sources of water realistically mimic what montane-dwelling herps would naturally encounter in the wild, but they also add to the relative humidity of the montane environment. As water vapor slowly evaporates from these water dishes, the relative humidity in the montane terrarium will stay correspondingly high: 60 to 70 percent relative humidity is best.

Speaking of humidity, keep things more or less moist depending on the herp species you house. A Mandarin rat snake, for example, does well with relative humidity of 60 to 65 percent, and it does not like perpetual dampness. Thus, plenty of dry space with damp or humid air is best for this species of colubrid. A Pacific giant salamander, on the other hand, enjoys high relative humidity and a continuous dampness in some parts of its habitat. This salamander needs to be able to travel from wetter to drier areas depending on its mood and needs at the moment.

No matter what species of herp you keep in your montane terrarium, always provide the animal(s) with dry places in which to escape the moisture of the tank. A dark cave, a dry hideaway, or a generally drier portion of the tank will serve this purpose because no species of terrestrial herp will thrive if it is wet *all* the time. Denying this dry area to your herp is inhumane and cruel, and it can lead to serious health problems down the road.

Because of the relatively high level of humidity that must be maintained in the montane environment, ventilation and air circulation are also prime factors that the hobbyist must address and "get right" to successfully maintain this biome type. I recommend covering no more than one-third to one-half of a screen lid with an impermeable layer of glass or acrylic. This coverage allows some moisture to be retained within the terrarium while still allowing the lion's share of moisture to evaporate and clean air to enter the terrarium. Obviously, the exact coverage of your tank and the level of humidity retained therein will depend on the type herp you keep.

Despite the species of herp or invert you keep, the need for fresh air and circulation within the montane terrarium is always a priority. Just as is true with the woodland and

Top Ten: Montane Species

Some montane species are hardier and more easily kept than others, and some can be downright impossible to maintain in captivity. The following table consists of some of the most commonly available species of montane herps you're likely to encounter in the pet trade.

1. Mountain horned dragon *(Acanthosaura spp.)*
2. Pacific giant salamander *(Dicamptodon ensatus)*
3. Mandarin rat snake *(Elaphe mandarina)*
4. Emerald swift *(Sceloporus malachiticus)*
5. Carpathian newt *(Triturus montandoni)*
6. Moellendorf's rat snake *(Elaphe moellendorffi)*
7. Rough-skinned newt *(Taricha grannulosa)*
8. Crested newt *(Triturus cristatus)*
9. Fire salamander *(Salamandra salamandra)*
10. Russian rat snake *(Elaphe schrenki)*

jungle styles of terrarium, the montane habitat must be allowed to periodically dry and refresh its oxygen supply lest the recirculating moisture within it become stagnant, stale, and polluted with nitrogenous wastes.

Heating and Lighting

Because the montane habitat also needs to stay cooler than just about any other biome type, you must approach the issue of heating and lighting with caution. An overly hot terrarium can stress or even kill a herp that is accustomed to much cooler temperatures. The increasingly popular Mandarin rat snake enjoys ambient temperatures in the mid- to low-70s (21.7° to 23.9°C) with a basking spot that does not exceed 85°F (29.4° C). This basking spot needs to be very small because the bulk of the tank should remain toward the lower end of the temperature range.

Maintain a basking area with a 60 to 75 watt lightbulb situated all the way toward one end of the tank so that a definite thermocline is present within the terrarium. Use at least two thermometers to keep track of the temperature range within the enclosure. To ensure the overall comfort of your montane herps, keep the cool end of the terrarium no less than 12 to 14 degrees (6.5° to 7.8°C) cooler than the warm end of the tank.

The longer you maintain a montane habitat and the more you observe the behaviors of your pet herps, the more attuned you will be to the inner workings of the tank and the needs/desires of your pets. If, for example, your mountain horned dragon (another high-elevation lizard from Asia) spends all its time in the basking area and virtually never ventures into the cooler end of the tank, you should raise the ambient temperature inside the entire tank by a few degrees so that the lizard may be comfortable throughout its entire home. The opposite is just as true. If your herp stays as far away from the basking site as possible all the time, it's highly likely that the basking light is too hot for it to enjoy. Switch to a lower-wattage bulb or position the lamp further away from the terrarium so that the basking spot cools down by a few degrees.

Semi-Aquatic Terrarium

Now we move on to my favorite terrarium style. This is a style that I have long been building and experimenting with, and it is one of the styles that first got me

The gorgeous Mandarin rat snake can be housed in a montane terrarium, but it is a delicate snake best left to specialists.

interested in keeping and maintaining living terrariums so long ago. It is the swamp terrarium. Actually, this terrarium's alternate name, the semi-aquatic terrarium, is likely a more realistically applicable name for it because all swamps are semi-aquatic environments, but by no means are all semi-aquatic environments swamps.

The semi-aquatic terrarium gives, in my opinion, a tremendous degree of creative license to the hobbyist when it comes to construction and setup. I've seen shoreline tanks, river bank tanks, swamp tanks, bog tanks, and waterfall tanks, but I think the most attractive semi-aquatic terrarium I've ever encountered was a 40-gallon-tall (151-l-tall) tank that had absolutely no earthen substrate to speak of. The floor of the tank was covered in a layer of decomposing leaf and plant matter atop a thin layer of aquarium pebbles. All of this was a full 5 inches (12.7 cm) below a column of water. In the water grew duckweed, water lettuce, and water hyacinth, and out of the water jutted a plethora of driftwood branches. Within the watery depths of the tank lived a small alligator snapping turtle that dined on the goldfish and crayfish that shared his underwater abode. Within the uppermost reaches of the tank, which was heavily clad in Spanish moss, thrived a colony of four squirrel tree frogs.

When I initially saw this tank, I wondered why the tree frogs had no dry substrate on which to walk, perch, or hunt. After learning that in the wilderness of the Okefenokee Swamp these frogs naturally live in cypress trees that are growing directly out of the water,

Constructing a semi-aquatic terrarium in which the reptiles, amphibians, and fish are compatible is a true challenge. However, the result is beautiful and satisfying.

and that a squirrel tree frog may go its entire life without ever touching solid ground, I better understood the unique ecological balance of the terrarium. The turtle fed on fish/crustaceans, the tree frogs ate crickets that would instinctively climb the driftwood perches after being dropped into the tank (which made them easy pickings for the waiting tree frogs), and the terrarium's floral occupants absorbed their nutrients by processing the wastes out of the water column. It was a beautiful setup. While such a terrarium might not suit the needs or skill level of all hobbyists, such a uniquely curious setup proves that the semi-aquatic vivarium offers plenty of "elbow room" when it comes to creativity.

Enclosure

Begin your semi-aquatic terrarium by asking yourself "What size habitat do I want to build? How deep does the water need to be to suit the needs of my herps? Do I want more land in my tank, or do I want more water in my terrarium?" The answers to these questions will largely determine what size tank you need to purchase. If you want more land than water or shallow water in your tank, virtually any terrarium larger than 20 gallons (76 l) should suffice. Any terrarium smaller than that may be too small to accommodate all components of the semi-aquatic ecosystem. If, however, you need deeper water in your tank, or if you want more water than land in your terrarium, I recommend a larger tank, at least 40 gallons (151 l). If you have the space, a 125-gallon (473-l) or larger tank can be the basis of an absolutely astonishing slice of a semi-aquatic ecosystem.

Substrate

Once you have selected your tank, gather the components of your substrate mix. I always begin by placing a 1- to 2-inch (2.5- to 5-cm) layer of pea gravel and nonsilica-based sand in the bottom of the tank. Obviously this will not act as a drainage layer because most of the tank will be perpetually under water. This layer does act as a physical stabilizer, however. Most organic substrates are quite lightweight and buoyant in water. In the home semi-aquatic terrarium, these properties cause organic substrate that is seated directly on the base glass of the tank to shift and move; over time, your substrate bed can slip, settle, and eventually slide into the aquatic portion of the tank, making for a muddy, sloppy mess. Therefore, it's always advisable to seat a foundation of sand and stone at the bottom of the tank to act as a stabilizer for the rest of the substrate.

Next, add your substrate mixture. Many semi-aquatic environments in nature have highly acidic soil. By virtue of the low pH associated with many semi-aquatic habitats in nature, most plant species that will thrive in the home semi-aquatic terrarium will do well in substrates with correspondingly low pH. Construct a substrate layer, therefore, by mixing 1 part peat moss, 2 parts coir, 2 parts composting leaf litter, and 1 part orchid bark. Depending on the exact species of plants you intend to house, the peat moss component may be increased or decreased based on those plants' tolerance of low pH. Mix these components thoroughly and layer the substrate 5 to 6 inches (12.7 to 15.2 cm) deep along only that portion of tank that will become dry land. It is important that you not layer any substrate mixture along the portion of the tank that will be under water.

Once you've covered a good portion of the base layer with substrate mix, begin to construct an easy slope in the substrate; about a 30- to 45-degree angle will work. This

Top Ten: Semi-Aquatic Herps

1. **Red-eared slider (Trachemys scripta elegans)**
2. **Spiny softshell turtle (Trionyx spiniferus)**
3. **American bullfrog (Rana catesbeiana)**
4. **Plumed basilisk (Basiliscus plumifons)**
5. **Chinese water dragon (Physignathus cocincinus)**
6. **Matamata (Chelus fimbriatus)**
7. **Emperor newt (Tylototriton verrucosus)**
8. **Tiger salamander (Ambystoma tigrinum)**
9. **Red-spotted newt (Notophthalmus viridescens)**
10. **African clawed frog (Xenopus laevis)**

Aquatic Kits

Half-and-half conversion kits—prepackaged kits that convert standard-size aquariums into a half-land/half-water tank—are a great way for a younger or inexperienced hobbyist to establish a semi-aquatic terrarium. These kits, which are easily installed and which offer rivulets, waterfalls, caves, and a host of other artificial, yet semi-naturalistic features (the kits are often molded to resemble rocky or stony structures), are a great way to begin understanding how equal amounts of both soil substrate and water will behave in a terrarium environment. I highly recommend these items for beginning hobbyists.

Even though these kits may incorporate numerous artificial items, it's important to remember that the naturalistic terrarium is an ever-evolving thing, and as time passes and the hobbyist's skills at managing a semi-aquatic terrarium advance, the artificial components of the tank can be replaced by lush, living plants and a realistic stony shoreline.

gentle slope will eventually become the shoreline, so make sure that it's gradual enough that the type of herp you plan to house will be able to easily scale the shore and make the transition from water to land. Highly agile semi-aquatic herps, such as the red-bellied water snake, can scale the most treacherous and steep of rough or textured inclines with little to no problem, while the clumsy chicken turtle will require a much gentler, even slope if it is to escape the water portion of its terrarium.

When the substrate is layered as thickly as needed and you've sloped one end of it so that your herps will be able to come and go from the water at their leisure, the time has come to begin layering flat, rugged stones atop the slope of the substrate. By "rugged" here, I mean stones that will withstand the constant buffeting of the aquatic filter that you will soon place in the water end of the tank. These stones must not be sedimentary or soft (easily crumbled) because such weak stones will soon disintegrate and dissolve into the water.

Avoid using small stones for the construction of your shoreline as well because smaller stones are easily washed away by the movements of your herps. Use large, heavy, and preferably flat river rocks to build your shoreline. A solid, stable shoreline is integral to the long-term success of the semi-aquatic terrarium. Once you've found stones that will serve this purpose, begin layering them in shingle-like fashion starting at the bottom of the shoreline and working upward. Cover as much of the substrate layer as you possibly can

While turtles will fare well in a semi-aquatic terrarium, they will usually trample and consume the plants. A hatchling painted turtle (*Chrysemys picta*) is shown.

because any uncovered spots in the shoreline will result in organic substrate trickling out into the water column and clouding it or clogging your filter. A good method that I've found for this is to build a primary shoreline with large rocks, then go back and fill in any holes with smaller pebbles until you have a very tight, dense shoreline that is free of any large gaps or holes.

Plants

With the completion of the shoreline, it's time to anchor your land-dwelling plants. Using the in-substrate or eco-planting method (the in-pot method seldom works in the land portion of this environment), anchor your chosen species of plants as deeply in the substrate as is necessary, keeping in mind that much of this substrate will be perpetually waterlogged. For example, a plant species that must have moist, but not wet, roots, such as "marble queen" devil's ivy, should be anchored very shallowly in the substrate, above the line to which the water table will eventually rise. Other types of plants containing roots that can tolerate perpetual water, such as the arrow plant, may be anchored much more deeply in the substrate, below the line to which your water table will rise. I typically allow my water table to rise to no more than 3 inches (7.6 cm) below the surface of the substrate; this ensures that any shallow-growing plants will have plenty of substrate through which to send their roots that is not below the waterline. Philodendron, piggyback plant (*Tolmeia*), wandering Jew, arrowhead vine, and all varieties of pothos do well on the land portion of the semi-aquatic tank. Pothos, for example, typically will thrive to such an extent that it must be trimmed and held in check lest it overtake the entire terrarium.

Aquatic plants are an excellent addition to the semi-aquatic terrarium; they give this style of tank a uniqueness and beauty that cannot often be duplicated in other terrarium styles. Water lettuce, hyacinth, water lilies, duckweed, and myriad other aquatic plants not only will add beauty to your tank, but they will contribute significantly to the overall ecological balance of the terrarium. As biological agents (like waste, excretions, and old foods) break down in the water column, these plants will readily absorb and process the excess nitrogenous chemicals produced. This not only will clean the water of the tank, but by virtue of the water column continually flowing through the substrate of the tank as well, will clean and refresh the substrate. Living, thriving plants in the water column of your semi-aquatic terrarium will make a noticeable difference in its appearance, odor, and ecological balance.

Water

With these land-dwelling plants in place, you may begin adding water to your semi-aquatic terrarium. I advise using only bottled water (or perhaps well water) for this purpose. (See the chapter 6 for a full discussion of the reasons.) Pour the water into the open portion of the tank that is destined to be the aquatic section. Pour it slowly and gently because your newly established substrate and shoreline can wash away more easily than you might think under a hard, fast torrent of water.

Once the waterline reaches about 3 inches (7.6 cm) below the surface of the substrate within the dry-land portion of the tank, stop adding water. Next, add a fully submersible aquarium filter or a hang-on style aquarium filter, depending on the height and function of your terrarium. A low, long tank housing aquatic turtles can be fitted with a hang-on style filter, while a taller tank or one that sports aquatic snakes

or frogs, either of which could easily escape through the hole left at the top of the tank by a hang-on filter, should be outfitted with a fully submersible model. Terrariums housing tadpoles or other fully aquatic herps may be outfitted with an air-foam-style filter, which has no motorized action and which poses no risk to the fragile amphibians. Fit the filter with the appropriate filtration media (activated carbon, particulate filter, etc.) and turn

If you have a large semi-aquatic terrarium with strong lighting, give the hardy and beautiful water hyacinth a try.

it on. This filter must be turned on as soon as the water is added to the terrarium because water that is not made to circulate will quickly grow stagnant and tainted.

Ground Cover

With the water in the tank and the filter up and running, you can now focus your attention on the ground cover. By virtue of the terrarium supporting a continual water table, the ground cover in the semi-aquatic habitat isn't as important for keeping the substrate moist as it is for keeping your herps dry. Every species of semi-aquatic herp needs some place where it can leave the water and dry off. In the naturalistic terrarium, flat stones placed atop the land portion of the tank, thick stands of moss, or dense layers of composting leaves all work well to provide dry sanctuary for your herps. Make sure that these items are layered thickly and that the moisture of the substrate never soaks these items.

It's also a good idea to construct a hiding place atop some dry item in the tank so that your herps may enjoy both the dryness of the locale and the seclusion and safety of a hideaway. Constructing a small stone cavern atop a broad, flat rock would satisfy these criteria, as would placing a half roll of cork bark atop a thick stand of moss. By satisfying your herps' needs for seclusion and dryness, you'll ensure the long term health and happiness of your pets.

The Chinese evergreens are hardy plants that do well in high humidity, making them good choices for swamp and jungle terrariums.

Décor

Haul-outs or dry locations are another important aspect of the semi-aquatic tank. Most species of aquatic turtles love to bask in the sun, but they typically do so only on rocks, exposed logs, or other items protruding directly from the water. Some frogs and aquatic snakes share this behavior of basking only on items that are completely surrounded by water. To accommodate the natural basking inclinations of these herps, place several haul-outs in the water portion of your tank. These haul-outs either may be natural items such as inclines of driftwood or tall stones, or they may be manufactured items such as plastic lily pads or foam slabs made to both float and look like natural wood or stone. These

African clawed frogs are completely aquatic frogs that are active and hardy.

artificial haul-outs are manufactured by a number of companies and are available through any pet shop dealing in herps and herp products.

Heating and Lighting

As is true of most aspects of the naturalistic terrarium construction and maintenance, the intensity and type of basking light you employ in the semi-aquatic terrarium hinges directly on the types of plants and herps you keep. A tank hosting a colony of Cope's tree frogs (a nocturnal species) needs only enough lighting to ensure the health of the plants. The terrarium that houses a Chinese water dragon, however, needs to be flooded daily with intense, full-spectrum light because this lizard needs bright light and UV-B exposure. Turtles require a warm basking light and UV-B light over the haul-out. Learn about the lighting needs of your herps before building your terrarium so that you can be better prepared to offer them the lighting apparatus that best suits their needs in captivity.

Fully submersible aquarium heaters also can add substantial heat to your terrarium. Simply sink the heater in the water part of your tank and adjust the thermostat to your desired temperature—usually no higher than 80° to 83°F (26.7° to 28.3°C) is sufficient. Because such heaters are exposed heating coils covered only by a thin casing of glass, they can present a hazard to your herps. Wrapping your heater in a mesh screen (mesh heater sleeves are available from most pet shops) can help to prevent your herps from ever making direct contact with the heating filament. You also can hide the heater behind or inside some décor items as long as the water is able to flow freely around it.

Maintenance

Should the water column of your tank become polluted with wastes, you'll need to siphon out about half of the water and refill the pool. Siphon the pool and suck up as much organic "gunk" as you can from the water column without disturbing the base rocks or substrate layers. This fouling of the water will happen early on in the terrarium's life but will become less frequent as the terrarium's ecosystem matures.

Ten Terrarium Invertebrates

Not all our vivarium inhabitants need be herps. A wide variety of invertebrate species can make superior captives. Any one of these spineless wonders can up the creepy factor in your vivarium. Take note, however, that while many species of herps can be housed communally, invertebrates, with the exceptions of herbivorous millipedes and cockroaches, always must be housed individually. Inverts housed communally will almost always kill and eat one another.

As with the herps, do your research before purchasing an invertebrate. Most species, including those from savannas and deserts, will require a humidified shelter. Others may have particular needs which may make them unsuitable for the exact terrarium you have created. Additionally, make sure you are getting the species you want, instead of a highly venomous but similar-appearing species.

Species	Vivarium Type
Goliath bird-eater tarantula *(Theraphosa blondi)*	Jungle
Mexican red-kneed tarantula *(Brachypelma smithii)*	Savanna
Pink-toed tarantula *(Avicularia avicularia)*	Jungle
Rose-haired tarantula *(Grammostola rosea)*	Savanna
Death's head cockroach *(Blaberus craniifer)*	Jungle/Woodland
Hissing cockroach *(Gromphadorhina portentosa)*	Jungle/Woodland
Emperor scorpion *(Pandinus imperator)*	Woodland
African black millipede *(Scaphiostreptus parilis)*	Jungle/Woodland
Tanzanian centipedes *(Scolopendra* spp.)	Jungle
Vietnamese giant centipede *(Scolopendra subspinipes)*	Jungle

Any rampant algae that are growing on the walls of the pool portion of the tank also may be scrubbed off with soap and a chemical-free sponge. Siphon as much water as you need to. Gently refill the pool with bottled water. Repeat the siphon/refilling steps if necessary to remove all the organic debris from the water column. As your tank matures, the plants will be able to better process the odor-causing wastes in the water column and you will need to siphon far less frequently.

Well, dear reader, there you have it. We've covered a lot of material and we've discussed a wide range of naturalistic terrariums, their construction and maintenance, and what sort of components go into each terrarium type and how those components will react with one another and with the ecosystem of your tank as a whole. If you've read this far, I'd like to congratulate you and urge you to keep reading magazine articles, online forums, editorials, and as many books as you can find on the topic of naturalistic terrariums. As much as I'd like to tell you that my book is perfect and that it's all you'll ever need to establish a perfectly healthy and functioning naturalistic terrarium, I can't say that.

Conclusion

It simply isn't true. No matter how good and no matter how thorough a book is, the truth of the matter is that no single source ever has all the answers about an issue. It's up to the hobbyist to seek out all the valuable information he can.

The care and maintenance of the naturalistic terrarium is nothing short of an art form; the more knowledge and firsthand experience you get on the matter, the better and more skilled you will become. With hard work and dedication, the simple, basic naturalistic terrariums you build today will, in time, be replaced by the elaborate, intricate self-contained ecosystems of the future. I wish you and your herps many happy and healthy years together in or out of your naturalistic terrarium.

CLUBS & SOCIETIES

Amphibian, Reptile & Insect Association
23 Windmill Rd
Irthlingsborough
Wellingborough NN9 5RJ
England

American Society of Ichthyologists and Herpetologists
Grice Marine Laboratory
Florida International University
Biological Sciences
11200 SW 8th St., Miami, FL 33199
Telephone: (305) 348-1235
E-mail: asih@fiu.edu
www.asih.org

Bromeliad Society International
6901 Kellyn Ln.
Vista, CA 92084-1243
E-mail: membership@bsi.org
www.bsi.org

International Euphorbia Society
Gardeners Cottage
Scampston
Malton, North Yorkshire
YO17 8NG
United Kingdom
E-mail: plantsman@tiscali.co.uk
www.euphorbia-international.org/index.htm

Society for the Study of Amphibians and Reptiles (SSAR)
The Claremont Colleges
925 N. Mills Ave.
Claremont, CA 91711
Telephone: 909-607-8014
E-mail: mpreest@jsd.claremont.edu

WEB SITES

Herp Digest
www.herpdigest.org

International Sansevieria Society
http://www.sansevieria-international.org/index.htm

Kingsnake.com
http://www.kingsnake.com

Reptile Forums
http://reptileforums.com/forums/

The Reptile Rooms
http://www.reptilerooms.org/

Setting up a Vivarium
http://badmanstropicalfish.com/vivarium/vivarium.html

The Vivarium Page
http://home.earthlink.net/~kenuy/vivarpage.htm

MAGAZINES

Reptilia
Salvador Mundi 2
Spain-08017 Barcelona
E-mail: Subscripciones-subscriptions@reptilia.org

Reptile Care
Mulberry Publications, Ltd.
Suite 209 Wellington House
Butt Road, Colchester
Essex, CO3 3DA
United Kingdom

Reptiles
P.O. Box 6050
Mission Viejo, CA 92690
www.animalnetwork.com/reptiles

Photo Credits: